Walks along the Lower Wear

Bill Hodgskin
&
Edwin Allen

Printed and Published by TUPS BOOKS
30 Lime St, Newcastle upon Tyne, NE1 2PQ
Tel: 0191 2330990   Fax 0191 2330578
ISBN 1-901237-08-7

INTRODUCTION

Encouraged by the success of their first book, *Walks Around Beamish Valley,* and their love of the North East countryside, Bill Hodgskin and Edwin Allen have put together what they call 12 enjoyable exercise walks.

All can be taken along or close to the river Wear as it winds 37.5 kms/23.3 mls. from the ancient city of Durham to the new city of Sunderland and out into the North Sea.

Each Walk can be accomplished within a few hours and all are in easy reach of the most populated areas of Wearside and Tyneside. They can be reached from further afield by using the A1M motorway or the A19 trunk road.

Designed to appeal to the individual or family walkers taking their first countryside walk as well as to the more experienced, these walks are intended to "get you up, about and exercising" in the lovely countryside that abounds along the river Wear.

Bill and Edwin believe that walking is the cheapest form of exercise you can take.

SO WHY NOT TRY IT, AND ENJOY IT!

When through the woods and forest glades I wander

and hear the birds sing sweetly in the trees,

when I look down from lofty mountain grandeur,

and hear the brook and feel the gentle breeze......

(from the hymn *How Great Thou Are*)

PUBLISHERS' NOTE

While every care has been taken in the compilation of this book, the publishers cannot accept responsibility for any inaccuracies. Things may have changed since the book was researched and published - paths are sometimes diverted, a concrete bridge may replace a wooden one, stiles disappear.

Public rights of way are constantly under threat, for various reasons. By following the walks in this book you can do your part in keeping these paths open to the public.

CONTENTS

ACKNOWLEDGEMENTS

We would like to express our deepest thanks to Amanda Allen for making sense of our notes enough to be able to type up the draft and final copies of the manuscripts into readable form.

Thanks once again to Gavin Hodgskin for his sketch interpretations of Edwin's photographs.

We thank our wives Joan and Jean for their tolerance throughout the time it has taken to research and compile these twelve walks.

Our thanks are also due to the following:

Peter Bell	Sunderland Countryside Officer (Environment Department)
Andrew Bewick	Sunderland Countryside Officer (Environment Department)
Clive Cromton	Logo
W.C. Fawcett	Caldecotes Walks (Author)
Mr. Grey	Low Barmston Farm, Washington
Dorothy M. Meade	Kepier Hospital (Author)
Mr. A.C. Newton	Animal Myths of Co. Durham (Author)
John Parkin	Great Lumley (History of)
Flora Pearson	Durham New College, Art & Design Department (for support and guidance of the sponsor pamphlet)
Mr. Kent Pedder	of Fatfield (hanging tree at Lumley Information)
St.Peters Vicarage	Background information to Saint Peters Church
Michael Richardson	Durham
Staff of Durham Ref. Library	for their help and patience during our research
Trevor Robertson	Tyne and Wear Development Corporation
Mr. J. Wood	Washington Ref. Library, for seeming to know what we were seeking when we were not sure ourselves.
Mr. Stokoe	Chester Diaries (suggestions about Virgin Well)
John Lowerson	County Secretary, Durham Scout County (background to Moorhouse Scout Camp Site)
Vicky Bell & Victoria Muir	Durham New College, 1st Year Art & Design Students, for the original design of the sponsor pamphlet.
T.J.C. Barling	National Trust Land Agent.

All those at County Hall Durham, too numerous to mention, who guided and advised us during the preparation of this book.

KEY SYMBOLS

═══════	Minor Road
- - - - - -	Public Footpath
◄───────	Route Direction
②	Location Point
⬆	Way Sign Green/Yellow
⌣⌣	Road Bridge
Ⓟ	Parking Area
i	Information
＼•／	Viewpoint
FB	Foot Bridge
PH	Public House

Places of Interest

Examples:	AW	Alice Well
	FC	Ferry Crossing

Comfort is essential to the enjoyment of any walk, so wear sensible footwear.

A leisurely pace is a comfortable pace and the walks in this book have been calculated at roughly 2kms (1mile) per hour to allow enough time for even the least experience walker to complete the route.

To obtain the best from your walks the sketch maps should be used in conjunction with the appropriate ordnance survey pathfinders 550, 562, 572, 2 inches to 1 mile, 4 cm to 1 km.

POINTS OF INTEREST
SUNDERLAND RIVERSIDE (ST. PETERS)

The Tyne and Wear Development Corporation

The Corporation was set up in 1987, with the aim of raising and investing millions of pounds in an effort to regenerate specific areas of both rivers left derelict after the demise of the shipbuilding and other heavy industries.

One of those sites lay on the North side of the Wear: Saint Peters/ North sands, Monkwearmouth, shipyards. Here the famous Empire Line Liberty ship was designed and built. It was adopted by the U.S.A. and Canada, and over 2,700 were built. These ships helped keep the lifeline open for Britain during the 1939-45 war.

The decision was taken to reclaim the land and build a mixture of housing and business premises, along with what is now the City of Sunderland's University campus and a National Glass Centre. Further 'attractions' were to be added in the future.

Along with these developments, there was the re-modelling of the North Docks into a Marina, with additional facilities including a Marine Leisure Activities Centre and a base for the R.V.L.I. Lifeboat, which is moored in the marina. All this is to be surrounded by housing developments around the marina.

New paths and wide promenades would run round and through the whole development, from North Docks to Bonners Field under the Wear Bridge and hopefully beyond.

The Sculptures

It was decided to enhance the project with a series of sculptures to be created for particular sites around the redevelopment. St. Peter's Riverside Sculpture Project came into being as an active partnership between the community, the main funder (Tyne and Wear Development Corporation), and the sponsor, Northern Rock Building Society, with the Artists' Agency as manager.

Sculptor Colin Wilbourn was appointed December 1991, soon to be joined by trainee Karl Fisher. Later they were joined by artist

1

blacksmith Craig Knowles, with crime writer Chaz Brenchley to contribute textual elements to the sculptural features.

While Colin and Karl would work in stone Craig would, as his title suggests, be working in metal, contributing to sculptures and making his own individual pieces. The sculptures and metal work are too numerous to go into detail in this book. There is a map/guide available from libraries, tourist information centres and the Artists' Agency (details at the end of this section).

Throughout the project Colin Craig and Karl have consulted and worked with local residents. For example, with Colin's and Karl's help, local schoolchildren designed and carved brick panels in the wall on the east side of the marina and made clay models of sea creatures which Craig translated into metal for the playground gate. This involvement was to help them take an interest and hopefully a pride in their area.

The artists' team want you to look at and enjoy their works, which I am sure you will; "Art is not for the special few, but anyone, be they postman or brain surgeon", to quote Colin.

St. Peter's Church

The church, which gives its name to the area, was built in A.D.674 by Benedict Biscop, on land given to St. Cuthbert to build a church and monastery. Only the west wall and porch remain of the original building, which was one of the oldest seats of learning in England, along with its sister church and monastery of St. Pauls at Jarrow on the River Tyne.

St. Paul's was built some seven years after St. Peter's and is much more closely associated with the Venerable Bede. However, Bede, who joined the church at a very early age - some sources suggest at only seven years of age - spent a great deal of his life at St. Peters, transferring to Jarrow only in later life.

The building of St. Peter's, with its stained glass windows, was unique in that Biscop brought Frankish masons and glaziers from Gaul for the first time. This meant the glass was made 'on site' instead of being imported as it had been previously. Sadly only a small sample of this original glass survives today, but it is on display inside the church (ask to see it).

Even today the stained glass windows, each with its own story to tell, are a credit to the church, as are the "Kneelers" in between the rows of pews. All of them are hand-embroidered, with a nautical, shipbuilding or Christian theme, by the ladies of the regular congregation.

In 1984 the church was the subject of an arson attack, and only the prompt action of the local fire brigade contained the main damage to the chancel roof. Even so, it was a costly fire.

The Victorian roof, without nails, was rebuilt and re-painted in its original colours. Over four thousand sheets of gold leaf were required, bringing the cost of the painting alone to over £13,000.

An excellent "potted" history pamphlet on the church is available from the church for a nominal sum, and is well worth obtaining, as are the services of the church guides, who are only to willing to show you around and answer any questions you may have.

St. Peter's Church, Monkwearmouth

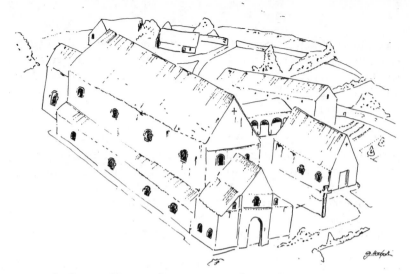

St. Peter's Church and Monastery, in the eighth century

The church is open every afternoon from 2.00 p.m. till 5.00 p.m. between Easter and October. (Details from the vicarage on 0191 567 3726; groups must book in advance.)

Before you leave this lovely old church, stand in the grounds and look towards the river, you will then become aware of standing on one of the oldest sites of Christian learning, while looking at one of the newest.

The Sunderland University Campus

When complete, the campus will form a large part of the infrastructure of the development of the St. Peters project. It will consist of a School of Business Studies in two buildings and a School of Art, Design and Communications in a third. As well as these, there are a Conference Centre and a National Glass Centre.

Because of Sunderland's long and close association with the glass industry, what better choice of sites for such a prestigious national facility of this kind than here, where glass making would appear to have started in Britain, at St. Peter's church (AD674) and next to the country's newest University campus.

A total of 88 architects sent in entries to a Europe-wide competition for the best design for the building. This was run by T.W.D.C. in

4

conjunction with the Royal Institute of British Architects.

The winner was London-based Gollifer Associates, who designed a bold, vast expanse of glass with a sweeping roof like the deck of a aircraft carrier. It has been described as a new landmark and lighthouse for culture and industry.

Costing some £15 million to build, it will provide business premises for Sunderland's still thriving glass industry, with facilities for up and coming glass crafts, workshops, and studios, and a permanent exhibition of both local and imported glassware.

It is hoped to attract around 75,000 people a year, all this on a 3 acre site, right on the river's edge, with easy access for able and disabled persons.

River and Bridges

Looking at it today, it is hard to imagine that until only a few short years ago the river was a busy shipbuilding and repair centre, with the honour at one time of producing more tonnage than any other shipping facilities in the world.

Shipbuilding was not the only industry, There were glassworks, ropers, coal and a host of others, all within a mile or two of the river's mouth, which until the 18th century was little more than a

Sunderland Bridge

muddy creek, kept partially dredged by horses and buckets working from the banks.

Crossing was only possibly by toll ferries until 1796, when the first iron bridge, sponsored by Roland Burdon M.P., was built. This was replaced in 1859 by a second, built by Robert Stephenson, and the present structure was erected over the river in 1929, this one designed by Mott, Hay and Anderson.

These bridges took the traffic away from the route through South and North Hylton. In 1974 a new bridge was built to carry the A19 trunk road over the river at Hylton, thereby relieving the heavy congestion that modern-day traffic had brought to Sunderland's city centre.

Another bridge was built alongside the Monkwearmouth/Sunderland road bridge in 1879, when it was decided to extend the railway across from Monkwearmouth Station, which had been built in 1848 as the terminus of the line from Gateshead, the journey into Sunderland having to be completed either on foot, or, for those rich enough, by hansom cab.

The station was commissioned by George Hudson (The Railway King), to mark his election as M.P. for Sunderland in 1845. This is why it is more impressive than one would expect for such a small place as Monkwearmouth.

A local man Thomas Moore (1791-1869) was chosen to design the building. Moore started from rather humble beginnings but worked his way up from being a joiner to become the architect not only of some of Sunderland's finest buildings, but also of others throughout the North East of England. It is unfortunate that he specialised in theatres, of which very few still exist today.

The station at Monkwearmouth, however, still survives, not in its original role but now a Museum of Transport. Good use has been made of the space available, exhibits not only of railway history, but also of other forms of transport through the 20th century.

At one time, at least 100 people were employed to run the place as a railway station and goods depot. It had its own station-master for 80 years, (Mr. James Brown being the last in 1927. After him the administration was carried out from Sunderland Central until it closed in 1967. Trains still use the line and bridge on their journey from Newcastle, but don't stop at Monkwearmouth.

The museum is open throughout the year except Christmas and Boxing day, and admission is free. Don't forget to pick up the free quiz and Information leaflets, which give you more details of the station's past history.

The Marine Activities Centre

This stands at the head of the marina, a four storey, grey/white building which is home to a range of organisations and facilities, including the Sea Scouts, Wear Boating Association, Sunderland Foy Boat Men and a Watersport project.

Alongside the main building are the Royal National Lifeboat Institute facilities and the Police Dogs unit. There is a small shop at ground level, and Raffiali's Flyin' Pizza restaurant is on the top floor.

The Centre also has as a central exhibition, a 'Tufa'. This is an outcrop of limestone, formed from the spring water which cascades down what was the cliff face.

Almost destroyed when the M.A.C. was being built, this natural formation has been strengthened, and the Hancock Museum (Newcastle) has prepared an information board which is situated beside the "Tufa". To view, just ask at the desk on the ground floor (access from the car park).

The Marina

The Marina is home to a variety of small craft, both leisure and working, each with its own moorings and pontoons for access.

You can see stationed there see the RNLI boat, which covers an area from Marsden to Blackhall rocks. At the time of writing the boat was the 'WAVELY LINE' 44017, a 17-year-old, 44 ft., Wavely class boat, with a five-man crew. This boat was however replaced by the newest 'Trent' class in March 1997. This is a much larger boat with more range and safety.

There is an invitation for you to knock on the RNLI door at any time. Providing some-one is available, they will answer any questions you may have. (Don't forget the collection box!)

Before leaving the Rescue services, you may be interested to have a look round a little museum at the top of Pier View. It is the headquarters of the Sunderland Volunteers Life Brigade, open to the public on Sundays only, from 12.00 midday until 6.00 p.m., throughout the year, or at any other time on request by ringing 0191 529 2651.

A snack bar and refreshments are available on Sundays. Admission is free, but they would welcome any contribution you may wish to make.

Places to Eat

A quick snack, a pizza or something more substantial, all are available within the boundaries of this walk.

The Bungalow Cafe

This is situated at the top of the Pier View with its entrance facing Roker Terrace and next to The "Wear Trail" information board.

This little cafe has a fine view over the harbour mouth, and is just the place to call into if you have the family with you, while just along Harbour View, in the direction of the Monkwearmouth Bridge, stands the Wolsely Hotel, which serves meals and bar snacks. However, be warned: it is best avoided on days when Sunderland F.C. are playing at home, as it is a favourite for supporters on their way to the match.

So why not cross the road and try Raffeali's 'Flyin' Pizza, which is located on the top floor of the "Marina Activities Centre", with access via a concrete walk-over, from Harbour View or the lower entrance of the centre next to the Marina. Bon Appetit.

Map and Information Leaflet

Available from Sunderland Tourist Office, Crowtree Road.
A 32 colour brochure all about the St. Peters Riverside Sculpture Project is available for £2.50 + £1 postage, from:- Artists Agency, 18 Norfolk Street, Sunderland, SR1 1EA.
Tel: 0191 510 9318 Fax: 0191 565 2846

SUNDERLAND RIVERSIDE (ST. PETERS)

Distance: 6 km/3 1/2 miles

Walking Time: 1 1/2 hours

Conditions: Paved walkways/steep steps x 2

Pathfinder: 550

Grid Ref: 369575

**** Parts of this walk are suitable for disabled persons

Starting from the Bungalow Cafe, which is tucked into the corner of Roker Terrace (1) at the top of Pier View after parking (if you come by car) in any one of the numerous car parks around the area; this walk will take you through a section of the river which has seen one of its most dramatic changes since the industrial revolution.

While both banks are being re-developed, the North has been completely transformed.

Where once ships were built and repaired, now stands the city's new University Campus and Business and National Glass Centres, as well as new housing.

Along with paved promenades, accessible to the public as part of the "Wear Trail", a series of pathways can be found on both sides of the river.

Walk down Pier View and follow the path around the outside of the "North Dock" housing estate (2). Continue following the path, keeping water to your left hand as you skirt around the Marina.

Walking around towards the M.A.C. you have on your right hand a brick wall with sculptured windows, designed by local schoolchildren and Monkwearmouth Local History Group.

Simply follow the paved walkway around the Marina, passing the Marina Activities Centre as you do so.

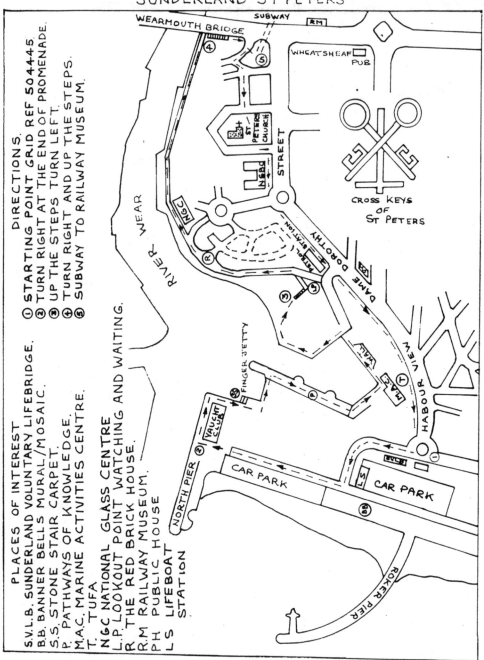

If you have time, go up the steps and into the building and ask at the desk to be allowed to see the "Tufa".

This is an outcrop of natural limestone, which has built up over centuries on what was the cliff face, where a spring pours out of the ground. It was rediscovered and identified as a "Tufa" when the Activities Centre was being built.

Next to the Activities Centre is the RNLI, where, if you are interested in the workings or background of the lifeboat and its crew, you may knock on the door and will find you are most welcome.

Walking on along the paved footpath around the marina, you are taken around the housing of "Fishermans Wharf".

Keep along the edge of the river and past the slipway, until you see the children's play area over to your right. Head for this, noting the sculptured iron gate at its entrance.

In front of you, running up the embankment is a series of 60 steps (3), which you need to climb; then a further seven to the project called "Watching and Waiting".

Continuing on the walk means following the tarmac path which runs behind the filling station and in front of the houses.

Easy to follow, this path slopes gently down to the river once more, passing as it does the first of the red sculptures, easily overlooked as it appears to be a section of broken wall. This is followed by the chimney pot, before you reach the Red House.

Leaving this, the path divides into two. Take the left route down to the river's edge.

The beautiful glass building on your right is the National Glass Centre, one of the major features of the St. Peters site.

Walk on along the wide paved promenade, passing the University Campus buildings as you do so.

This was the first stage of the campus which was opened by Egon

The Red House, St. Peter's Quayside

Kletsch, president of the European Parliament in 1995. Across the river stand the new student accommodation and Sunderland's small fish quay.

As you walk along this broad paved promenade, you come to what looks like a concrete block left over from a building site, which in a way it is, because, if you take notice as you approach it, there is a bollard set on top. This was once a block for tying ships to, when the site was a shipbuilding and repair yard. It is now the only reminder of that era.

Walking on takes you past a brick building set slightly higher up the bank side. This building has had many uses in the past, including a restaurant, but now consists of offices.

At the end of this building a small park-like area sits between it and the bridge, known as Bonners Field.

Once you reach the base of the bridge (4), for the sake of this walk you now have 121 steps to climb (did we miss any?).

If however you wish to, you can continue along the path under the bridges, and through the concrete arched avenue.

It will take you further up river, as far as the new Sunderland Football Stadium. However, you need to retrace your steps back to the bridge, as the path comes to a dead-end at a point where the staithes for Monkwearmouth pit once stood. This takes approximately another 30 minutes to complete and there really is very little worth seeing (except the luxury pigeon lofts).

Once you have climbed the steps, stopping to take in the view of the river and St. Peters walk, turn away from the bridge and walk down to the Tyre Services warehouse on the corner.

At the corner, you will see, across the road, the entrance to the subway (5) which leads you, should you so wish and have the time to spare, to the Monkwearmouth Railway Station Museum.

From outside the tyre warehouse walk away from the main road, down the hill, past the entrance of the office block which you passed on the river's edge.

Here you cross the road. Watch out, it's not as quiet as it first appears.

Walking up the street on the other side, you come to Charles Street and Bonners Field industrial units. At the end of this street you can see St. Peters Church.

Lookout point

13

Take the path through the church yard, and please do try to find the time for a visit, we are sure you will not be disappointed (see local interest section for times). There is usually some one there to give a guided tour.

The churchyard path comes out at the east end, close to the vicarage.

Out of the gate, turn left, cross the road and walk up to the main road, turning right once you reach it.

Now here we must apologise for taking you along a rather busy road, but in this way you will be able to see some of blacksmith Graig Knowles' work, the gates into the back of the Business Centre (what about those bicycles?).

As you pass the top of the road leading down to the harbour the road changes its name from Dame Dorothy Road to Harbour View, and this is exactly what you get, by taking the footpaths close to the edge. There are even seats provided to allow you to sit and admire the vast changes that have taken place along this stretch of the river.

From here, it is only a short walk to the top of Pier View and the Bungalow Cafe and the end of your walk.

If you still have time and they are open, why not look in at the Sunderland Volunteer Life Brigade House, just down past the shelter on Pier View? (see local interest section for details)

POINTS OF INTEREST
SOUTH HYLTON/OFFERTON HAUGH

It is hard to believe today that at one time the area around North and South Hylton was a hive of industry, with John Wigham's slipway and engineering works, paper mills and cement works on the South bank alone.

Public House

Surrounded by working men's houses was the original Golden Lion Inn. As far as our research can tell, the inn was built in 1705. This is borne out by the Hylton coat of arms and the initials J.D.H. 1705, carved on a plaque which rests above the entrance.

This same plaque can now be seen above the present inn, which was built in 1912 a little to the west of the original.

Greatly improved since Tetley's Breweries purchased it in March 1987, the inn now has a large conservatory which, like the rest of the interior, is tastefully decorated.

It not only caters for larger or special functions, but also serves meals and bar snacks in the homely comfort of the bar and lounge areas, along with a wide selection of fine ales.

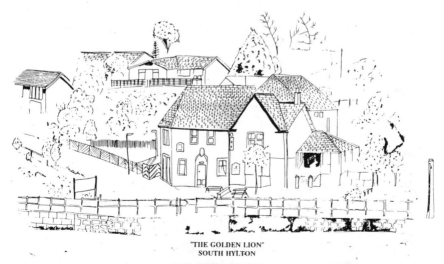

"THE GOLDEN LION"
SOUTH HYLTON

SITE OF OLD FERRY CROSSING

Ferry and Bridges

Looking around the interior walls you can find some excellent and interesting old photographs portraying the area in its heyday, when it stood on the main route between Sunderland and Newcastle.

That was until 1796, when a bridge, promoted by Roland Burdon (MP for Durham), was constructed across the river, near the mouth, connecting Sunderland and Monkwearmouth.

This had the effect of diverting traffic through Sunderland, and was obviously much quicker means of travel than having to wait for the ferry.

The ferry itself was a chain-operated, flat-bottomed craft with very limited capacity, slow and not altogether safe.

It did survive however for a good number of years, probably more as a passenger than a vehicle ferry until 1957 when it carried the last fare across the river. But it was to be nearly 20 years - in 1974 to be exact - before traffic would cross the river at this point once more, this time by bridge.

To alleviate the problems of traffic passing through Sunderland on its way South or North, it was decided to build a new trunk road. This was to become the A19.

Keeping well clear of the town as it was then, it linked with the tunnel under the Tyne and passed over the Wear by means of a box-girder bridge, between North and South Hylton.

Designed by R. Tavers Morgan, as is the Chatershaugh bridge higher up the river, it towers above you as you walk beneath it, a monument to today's engineers.

Copperas Gill

Copperas Gill is the stretch which you climb on your way towards the Wearside Golf Club, and gets its name from the works which existed along this stretch of the river in the 19th Century.

Copperas and Ferrous Sulphate (also known as Green Vitriol), were obtained from the iron pyrites taken from coal waste and mixed with rainwater. When matured, the copperas was used for paper manufacture and dye-making in the hat industry.

It used to be said that to tell if the copperas was matured, you only had to drop an egg on to it, and it would shell the egg if matured Whether the egg was raw or boiled is not recorded.

Old Railway

The section of disused railway, now part of Sunderland Wearside Trail, which runs between Wood House farm and the A19 flyover, is approximately 1.6 km/1 mile in length with a small cottage set approximately half-way along this section.

This is Railway Crossing Cottage, which as the name implies stood at the corner of a junction where a road ran across the railway.

In the cottage would live a "Crossing Keeper" and his family. It was his job to operate the gates, allowing trains through while stopping the road traffic.

Then once it was safe to do so, he would open up the gates to allow the road traffic free passage.

Now the cottage is just a home, with its neat gardens, a reminder of days gone by, when the railway line was alive with passenger and freight trains.

Once again, nature is taking over, and with help from the Sunderland Environmental Department, this is becoming a pleasant track for walking and taking exercise at any time of the year.

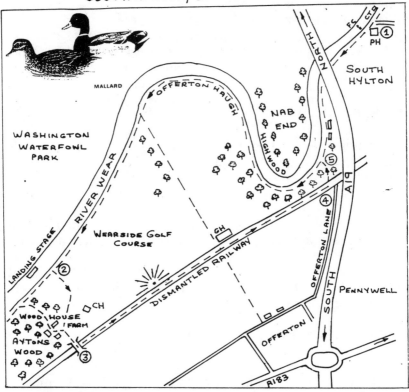

① STARTING POINT OPPOSITE "GOLDEN LION" INFORMATION BOARD GRID REFERENCE 352569.
② TURN LEFT AT COPPERAS GILL.
③ DOWN THE STEPS TURN LEFT PENSHAW/PALLION PATHWAY.
④ TURN LEFT DOWN THE STEPS TO RIVERSIDE.
⑤ TURN RIGHT AT RIVER PATH.
PH PUBLIC HOUSE GOLDEN LION.
CT CONCRETE TUG.
CH CLUB HOUSE WASHINGTON GOLF CLUB.
GH OLD RAILWAY GATEHOUSE.

Golden Lion, South Hylton, Site of old ferry crossing

SOUTH HYLTON/OFFERTON HAUGH

Distance: 6.6 km/4.1 miles

Walking Time: 1 3/4 hours

Conditions: Dry paths, one incline/steep steps

Pathfinder: 562

Grid Ref: 352 569

The walk starts from the public car park on the edge of the river Wear, opposite the "Golden Lion" public house in South Hylton (Sunderland, Tyne and Wear).

To gain access to this, come off the A19 at the A183 junction and head towards Sunderland. At the first roundabout, turn left, passing Dewhirsts factory on your right hand and the Sunderland Echo's office complex on the left.

The road passes through the rows of terraced houses which make up the Pennywell estate.

At the next roundabout turn left and continue down this road, through 'South Hylton' and down to the river.

The road terminates at the foot of the hill where the 'Golden Lion' stands.

At one side of the car park there is a large and very informative notice board (1) provided by Sunderland Council, and well worth looking at before you set off.

Also part of the old wooden derrick which was used for loading barges is still standing, next to the car park.

Once you are ready, take the path in the direction of the A19 fly-over, the steel and concrete bridge that spans the river where once the only method of crossing the Wear at this point was by ferry.

As you walk under the bridge, which was completed in 1975 as part of the major road restructuring programme, you will find to your left hand a derelict farm building.

Just beyond this and a little further around the bend in the river is a newer 'Dutch' style bungalow with stables, called 'Riverside Lodge'.

The path is broad and firm for the next few hundred yards, passing more houses, the last of these being 'Garden House'.

It is worth noting that because the Wear is for a good part of its length tidal, a fair amount of sea-weed and seagulls will be seen on its banks at this stage.

Once the end of the path is reached, at a point beside Garden House, it narrows down to a bridle path which follows the river, passing through a gap in a stone wall. On the far side of this stands a wooden plinth, with the Sunderland Countryside plaque set in the top.

It is then just a simple matter of following this path for the next 1.2 kms (three-quarters of a mile) or so, round the edge of Offerton Haugh.

Birds such as the common gull, crows and even cormorants can be seen feeding along the muddy banks at low tide.

At this point, across the river, lies 'High Woods', which is the setting for another of Sunderland's Countryside Walks, and is also featured in this book.

The path follows the river bank on one side and open fields on the other, and no matter what the weather is like, walking is dry. You will be able to see, where 'High Wood' ends and the wire fence around the 'Washington Waterfowl Park' begins.

At the end of this section you find yourself confronted by a stile, over which a broad path goes off to the left. Ignore this and continue along the river's edge, with the Wearside golf club to your left.

The path is firm as it winds its way through a wooded section and up an incline.

Near the top you will find a seat, and from here you can see on the far side of the river, the warehouse of the Asda supermarket chain, and, slightly to the left, at the river's edge, a pontoon for the Washington Wildfowl park.

From this point the path drops away down to the edge of the river once more. It is a simple matter of looking out for the "Countryside" path signs as you climb once more into the next woods.

Unfortunately the path, which was laid for walkers, is now being damaged by mountain bikes, their tyres pulling up the gravel to expose the softer sub-soil.

Follow the path until you reach the next seat, which stands next to the entrance to a private footpath leading off to the left. Here the path drops down again to the very edge of the river via a series of steps cut into the hill.

At the bottom you will find two "Way" signs, one is a wooden plinth with cobble-stones set around it, the other is a plain wooden post set in the ground.

From here you turn left and continue up the path as it climbs from the river, keeping the gully, known as "Copperas Gill", to your left hand (2).

At the top of this short but steep climb you will find a five-barred gate with a stile at one side. To the left stands another "Wayside" plinth.

Once over the gate, you find yourself on a broad tarmac roadway which leads down to the club house of Wearside Golf Club, on the left.

You however walk straight up the road, which is a public right of way, in the direction of the buildings on the right-hand side, these being Wood House farm.

A short distance from the white gates of the farm you reach the stone parapet of the old railway line, now a country walk.

It was at this point that the authors, who usually try to avoid these railway walks, as most of them are too bland, with very little scenery and too many cyclists, decided to give this one the benefit of the doubt, and were well rewarded.

To join the railway line, after stopping on the bridge for a break, note a signpost just to the right hand side of the road, directing you down the few steps on to it (3).

It is then just a case of turning left and walking under the bridge to continue your walk.

Within a few yards of the bridge is a small notice board which informs you that this is the Penshaw/Pallion pathway. It also contains snippets of information regarding the flora and fauna and the bird life you might expect to find along its length.

You will find it extremely popular with walkers, but do watch out for cyclists - the reason becomes more obvious as you ramble its length.

This section is set up along the hill side which runs down to the valley floor, with the river Wear running through it, so that a splendid view of the whole area lies before you.

Approximately half-way along this section, about 1.2 km (three-quarters of a mile) you reach a set of steel pipe barriers, set at the junction of what was once a railway crossing.

The original cottage, aptly named "Railway Crossing Cottage", still stands on one corner, and is still occupied, although the present tenants are no longer required to open and close the crossing gates, as would have previous occupiers when the line was in use.

There is a signpost which points down to the left, declaring, "River Wear 1/2 mile', and one pointing in the opposite direction. This one gives no destination, but in fact points to Offerton.

Continue straight on along the railway path for approximately the same distance again, until you can see you are approaching a rather busy roadway. This is of course the A19.

As you approach it, it becomes obvious that an archway runs under the A19, or to be correct, the road was built over the top of the railway. This allows the path to make its way into and through the Pennywell estate and on to the edge of Pallion.

You however are going to turn left off the path just before the arch and stables which stand to the right of it (4).

Watch carefully for the "Countryside" plinth set at the head of the steps, which lead off at the left-hand side of the path.

The series of stone steps (watch out as you walk down them) takes you down to the river path and opposite Garden House(5), which you passed at the start of the walk.

Re-trace your steps along this section, under the "Flyover" and back to the car-park opposite the Golden Lion, to finish what we hope has been a pleasant and interesting walk.

POINTS OF INTEREST
NORTH HYLTON/HIGH WOODS

A good part of this walk takes you through some of the finest oak woodlands in the North East of England. Recognised as a site of "Ancient Woodland", the landscape has changed very little since the last Ice Age.

While the woodland remains as it was then, the river banks have gone through what could be called a full circle from rural, into busy industrial, and now back to rural landscape.

There is still plenty of evidence of the area's industrial past, if you look carefully at the river banks. Old stone sections of quayside and ferry landings can still be seen.

Manor Farm

Manor Farm lies just beyond the A19 flyover. It was at one time, not only the centre for agriculture in the area, but also supported a thriving pottery industry (North Hylton Pottery), part of which can be seen in the shape of the large square chimney standing within the boundaries of the farm buildings.

Furthermore in 1910, Robert Welford, a resident of the farm, constructed an early type of mono-plane in the outbuildings. Whether it ever flew and from where does not seem to be recorded.

Wood House Farm/Quarry

Lying at the top of the incline and above Manor Farm, it had a very short industrial life, from about the middle until the end of the 19th century.

By then the quarry was overgrown and the steam winding engine at the farm had disappeared, leaving only the gully and brick arched bridge as reminders.

The gully was built to take a railway, powered by the steam winding engine, to transport sandstone from the quarry down to the barges that lay in the river. These barges then transported the stone down river to Sunderland and Wearmouth for building purposes.

Pathway to High Woods, North Hylton

High Woods

Because the woods have lain unaltered for so many years, they are naturally a haven for wild life, especially birds. Willow warblers, black-caps, woodpeckers and even robins can be seen feeding on the berries of the alder, ash and hawthorn that grow among the oaks.

In winter birds from Europe and Scandinavia find their way here to feed, away from the harsh conditions of their homelands.

Low Barmston Farm

This is a small cluster of buildings with the farm house standing a little to the north of the rest of the farm.

This house was built in 1840 as a wedding gift for the eldest daughter of the Earl of Durham (who built Penshaw Monument) by her father and was at that time very much in the 'back garden' of the Lambton Estates.

Her sister, the third daughter, married Earl Grey, of whom the monument and street in Newcastle are named in honour.

The Eastern Highway

Also known as Sunderland Highway, this was built as a major 'feeder' road, from the A19 trunk and A1231 Wessington Way from Sunderland, taking traffic into the heart of Washington, with its factories and offices, as well as to the shopping complex and leisure centre of the "Galleries".

The pathway which runs alongside the Eastern Highway, was part re-laid with dolomite, in 1995 by Sunderland City's Environment Department, and is an alternative route away from High Wood.

The Shipwright Arms

This is a traditional country riverside public house which can trace its history back nearly 350 years, to the days of sailing ships, pirates and press gangs (ask to see an original press gang cosh if you go in for a meal or drink). It is a listed building, but it is not haunted.

It is still known to the local population as "Swanees" after Mr. Swan, who was landlord for a good number of years. The car park at the side of the building was at one time a Fire Station with a horse-drawn engine, and before that there was here a Ship Chandlers which supplied sailing ships throughout the 17th, 18th and 19th centuries.

Shipwright Arms

Situated as it is, it was of course a coaching house on the way to and from Durham via the river road, with the ferry outside its door. You can still see the old ferry steps and landing on either side of the river, just west of the pub.

Part of the building was given over to the Post Office for a while and had the only telephone in the area during the Second World War.

Now managed by Maureen and Tony Atwill, both members of the British Institute of Innkeeping, this small but well maintained pub has a string of credits to its name. Mentioned in the "Good Food Guide", it is also a Vaux's Pub of the Year winners, and has been listed for 18 years in "Cameron's Real Ale Guide". It has been featured on local television and voted "Scran" Pub of the Month by the Sunday Sun newspaper.

A comprehensive menu of over 65 dishes, some vegetarian, with OAPs' and children's meals, is available and all reasonably priced. There is also a Sunday Lunch menu with a choice of meats. Bar meals are served Monday to Sunday lunchtimes 12 to 2.30 pm and Monday to Saturday evenings 7 to 9.30 pm. Please remember Maureen and Tony's advice: "Be patient at busy times, remember freshly cooked food takes a little longer to prepare".

Should you require accommodation, en-suite bed and breakfast is available and fully recommended by the Northumbria Tourist Board, of which Tony and Maureen are members. Should you wish to sample the menu at the Shipwrights and feel the need to telephone for a reservation the number is 0191 549 5139.

The Wessington, which stands next to the D.F.S. furniture store, is one of a newer generation of pubs being built to cater for children which may suit the family with younger children.

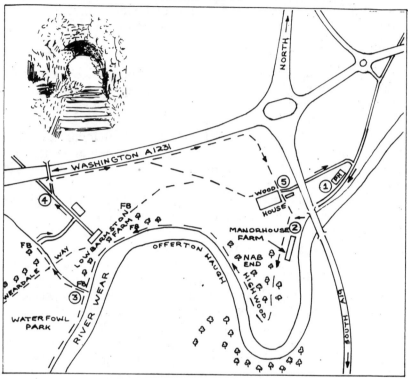

① GRID REF. 349569 PUBLIC HOUSE SHIPWRIGHT ARMS.
② TURN RIGHT AND UP THE STEPS.
③ TURN RIGHT AND FOLLOW PATH
④ TURN RIGHT AND FOLLOW PATH
⑤ TURN LEFT AND FOLLOW PATH UNDER A19

NORTH HYLTON/HIGH WOOD

Distance: 5.52 kms/3.42 miles

Walking Time: 2 hours approx.

Conditions: Hilly/woodland paths

Pathfinder: 562

Grid Ref: 349 569

The "Shipwright Arms" (1) public house, down by the river at North Hylton, is the starting and finishing point of this circular walk up through "High Wood", to Low Barmston, along the edge of the Eastern Highway and back down to the river by way of an underpass through the A19 trunk road.

As always, you would be advised, if you came by car, to park close to the public house, even though there are parking areas further along the path, for all the obvious reasons.

Leaving the "Shipwright Arms", you walk towards the concrete towers which support the bridge carrying the A19 over the River Wear.

Across the river to your left, towards the "Golden Lion" public house, you can still see parts of the old quayside, from which the passenger and vehicular ferries left to cross the river, this being the main route between Sunderland and Newcastle until a bridge was built in the 18th century, close to the river mouth at Sunderland.

The path you are on is more of a wide tarmac path which is used by the people who live in what is left of "Manor House", which lies on the bend of the river, just past the bridge.

As you approach this huddle of buildings, you pass what was built as a car park with a large information board in one corner. Unfortunately both car park and board have been badly vandalized, which is a great pity, because this is the start of a very picturesque walk.

Part of an old wall stands to your right, just as you reach the "Gully". This cut in the hill-side was used to lower stones from the quarry above to barges lying at the quayside for shipment down river.

A series of steps run up through the walled sides (2), passing through a brick arch at the top, which makes climbing much easier.

So it's up the steps and left turn at the top, on to a couple more wooden steps, through a small gate, to find a "Way" sign on the right and a wooden plinth bearing the "River Wear Trail" plaque on the top of it.

The path narrows down but remains very firm. Then veering right you will spot a second of the "Wear Trail" plaques.

Next you go up a series of six steps to where the path starts to run alongside a fenced-off field on the right and trees to the left.

These steps are the first of many that you will encounter throughout the section of the walk that winds its way through the woods. Behind the fence you can still make out the shape of the old quarry, and sitting almost on the far rim, "Wood House Farm".

It becomes obvious from the start why the area is called "High Wood", as you look down through the trees to the river below.

The old buildings, still inhabited, which you can see below through the trees on your left, are "Manor House", which sits on the edge of the river.

As you walk through the woods, especially in spring or early summer, you will not only find all the usual woodland flowers and trees but also wild cherries in full bloom.

The path is easy to follow as it rises and falls along the head of the woods, before it bends to the left and slowly drops towards the river once more.

Tree roots stick up through the path in parts, but do not present any problems on dry days, but take care in wet weather or after rain.

There are also short sections of the path which have been built up at the sides, using small logs, showing that some maintenance does get carried out from time to time.

Just before you start to descend, looking over to your left, across the river, you can see the path and houses that you pass should you decide to try the "South Hylton/Offerton Haugh" walk in this book.

Towards the bottom of the incline, over to your left again, on the side of the river, hidden in the trees and undergrowth, you can just make out the charred remains of some brick buildings - can you see them?

Then as the path veers right, you will find a tree which has fallen; the roots to the right of the path, while the trunk is over to the left, leaving the path clear.

A double wire fence to protect newly planted trees runs alongside the river, while grassy mounds stand on the opposite side of the path.

Once again if you look to the far side of the river, you can see evidence of old quaysides which were a regular feature of the area.

The path branching into two is the next thing you need to watch out for, and it is the broader, right hand one you follow, just before it starts to rise once again, away from the river's edge.

Along this section you pass through a passage-way made up of gorse bushes, which, when in full bloom in spring and summer, give the appearance of yellow walls.

Just after this, the path reaches the foot of a flight of steps, twenty in all, which you must climb before the next set of four, which takes you on to two wooden planks spanning a culvert.

Further on are another bridged culvert and another 20 steps (we did warn you!).

At the top of these stands the usual wooden plinth, but this time you may find it without the plaque, unless the council have replaced it before this book goes to press.

There is also a red arrow pointing out the trail you are following, with another pointing in the opposite direction.

Ignore the track leading off to the right, across the grass, and stick to the main path.

The next landmark is a footbridge and seventeen steps, which brings you to a section with a wire fence around a field. Take a right hand turn, go down four steps, cross another culvert and go up four steps. After this come more steps and another bridge, all within a few metres.

This pattern of steps and bridges repeats itself throughout the woodland section of the walk.

Look out for a green painted signpost set against the trees on your left. This points to Washington in one direction and North Hylton in the other. Because it stands at the foot of a series of steps running up into the woods, a "Way" sign is attached to the lower steps telling you that it is in the direction of the "Wearside Trail".

However, for the purpose of this walk, you will have no need to climb these steps, but will follow the signpost's directions to Washington.

As the path continues to follow the river there is a point where you can see the pontoon floating in the water next to the "Wildlife Park" - see it?

Then, just as you approach another bridge - this one has handrails - there is to your right another path, with "Way" signs and a carved notice board, giving details of the "Sunderland Woodland Trust".

You continue over the bridge, up the incline, past the concrete outlet pipe down to the left, until you reach the last steps.

These take you up the hill-side in zig-zag fashion, bringing you out against a fence, which goes around the field and stables of Low Barmston Farm, and the start of the chain fence around Washington Wildlife Park.

Just follow the path around the houses of the farm, until you reach the corner of the field. Here you turn sharp right, which will put you on to planks of wood spanning a small stream.

At the far side of this you find yourself standing on a "T" junction, with a signpost pointing to the right and stating "Bridle Path to Lower Barmston Farm" (3).

So turning right, follow this broad, dry path, past the lumps of concrete partly covering the pipe which is buried into the path.

Next is a bridge, which crosses the same small stream you passed a short distance back.

This bridge, unlike the rest of those you have encountered, is broad, made of iron and used by farm vehicles.

Beyond the bridge, as you are walking along, look over to your right. Here on a clear day you can see right across the valley to the far side, to "Railway Crossing Cottage", set on the Old Pallion/ Pelton railway line, and even to "Offerton", set higher up the hill. Can you see them?

At the end of this short stretch, you reach a barrier, above which stands a signpost telling you that the path from the "Wildlife Park" was created by funds from the Countryside Commission.

Walk around to the right of the barrier and you find yourself on a broad tarmac roadway, facing "Low Barmston Farm", at the far side.

Built in 1840 for the eldest daughter of the First Earl of Durham, Lord Lambton, as a wedding gift, it was considered to be in "the back garden of the Lambton Estate".

When standing facing the house, you see a garage type building of grey stone, with black doors, to the left, and to its left, a stile, with "Way" signs attached. This leads on to a path which will take you back down to "High Wood".

You however will walk past and continue up the tarmac path in the direction of the bridge which spans the A1231 (Eastern Highway).

Looking over to your left you can see the huge ASDA warehouse, built in 1994 to supply its superstores throughout the Northern Region.

A short stroll brings you to the foot of the bridge and a "dolomite" path on the right (4).

Just beyond the path is a signpost telling you that there is a public footpath to North Hylton, 2.4 kms/1$^1/_2$ miles away.

When the authors first tried this walk in the spring of 1995, this path had just been relaid thanks to the Environment Department of the City of Sunderland.

It is a good solid, dry path, making walking easy, and although it runs close to the main road, because it is set slightly below the road level, you will find it comparatively quiet, and after the "ups and downs", of "High Wood", it is worth what little noise there is, just to walk along a straight and level path.

The view on a clear day is another bonus when you follow this route. Once again you can see right across the valley, with the A19 running down to your left, and over to the right, the area where other walks in this book are located.

Keep following the path as far as the point where if you turned left, you would go into an underpass, instead turn right, over the stile and on to the tarmac path down the edge of the field.

This is a "Right of Way", so don't think you are trespassing (you will see it indicated further down the path).

A few hundred metres down stands a five-barred gate which looks as though it has not been closed for many a year past. The stile at the right hand side is no longer usable, but walking through the gate opening, you may spot the "Way" signs on the post.

Once through this, it is a short walk to the next one which leads into the yard of Wood House, which stands in front of you.

Take the stile at the left hand side, cross the yard and veer over to the left, in front of the house (5).

There is another stile straight across the yard, with "Way" signs attached. This takes you down to the river path, through the woods.

However, as stated, you go off to the left on to the tarmac path.

Remember that if you use the gate, and not the stile, leave it the way you find it open or shut.

The tarmac path slopes down towards an underpass, over which the A19 runs, and is dotted at various points with signposts detailing paths across fields, to the left.

Towards the foot of the hill the road as it now becomes, curves to the right and finally comes out at the car-park of the "Shipwright Arms" and of course the finish of your "High Woods" ramble.

We hope you have enjoyed it, and that it whets your appetite to try some of the other walks along the "Wear" featured in this book.

POINTS OF INTEREST
JAMES STEEL PARK

The James Steel Park is named in honour of the man who was Lord Lieutenant of Tyne and Wear 1974/1984 and Chairman of the Washington Development Corporation 1964/1977.

The Park was developed on land which had been left derelict with the demise of the industries which had once thrived in this area. Industries such as coal mines, stone quarries, ships and timber yards, along with the huge chemical works, dominated the sky line and polluted the area on the north side of the river close to Low Barmston.

As the new town of Washington got into its stride in the 1970's, the planners turned to the districts of Fatfield and Biddick, and new housing estates and factories rose up on land which once held communities like that of Low Barmston, with its huddle of working men's terraced houses constantly covered in grime from the old industries.

This was, however, a community which still boasted, a Wesleyan Chapel, a Mission Hall and two public houses, the Staithes Inn and the Foresters Arms, with a third, the Earl of Durham not half a mile away, close to the river's edge.

No fancy names adorned the streets of Low Barmston, no avenues or closes, just rows of houses such as "Blast Row", "Wilden Terrace" and "Middlefield Row".

All this was swept away with the new development, leaving space to create a cleaner environment for the people who still live in the area. And so the Park was born.

It extends for two-and-a-half miles on both sides of the river from Fatfield/Biddick in the West to Cox Green in the East.

There is still plenty of evidence of the area's industrial heritage, all along the river banks, where parts of old staithes and quays can still be spotted among the lush vegetation which grows along the river's edge.

In fact the whole area is full of interesting features, some of which we will expand upon in the following text, starting with the three bridges which span the River Wear within the parks boundaries.

The Biddick-Fatfield road bridge

The Road Bridge

The Road Bridge crosses the river from Biddick to Mount Pleasant.

Called the Biddick or Fatfield Bridge, this was originally built to carry what was at the time, the main road between Old Washington and Houghton. Designed and built by D. Balfour, it was opened in 1891 by the Third Earl of Durham.

A local story has it that the first vehicle across was a horse and cart carrying the body of a miner killed at the North Biddick Colliery.

The Rail Bridge

Better known as the Victorian viaduct, this bridge was built to the design of a Roman aqueduct at Alcantra in Spain. It is without doubt one of the most impressive of all the crossings on the river.

Erected for the Durham junction of the North Eastern Railway at a cost of £35,000, it opened on Queen Victoria's Coronation Day in August 1838, the 20th to be exact.

It was designed by Walker and Bruges, with a Mr. T.E. Harrison as the resident engineer.

Running a length of 249 metres, it measures 6.5 metres between parapets, with a total height, from the base of its foundations of 46 metres (above river level some 40 metres).

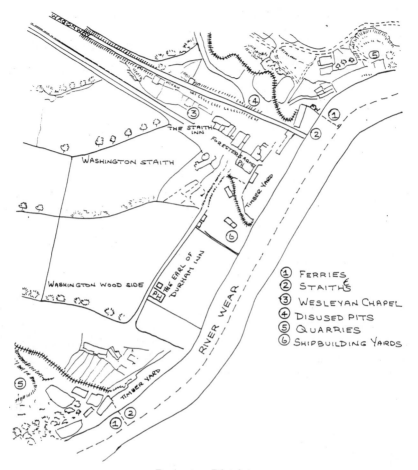

Barmston District

It is said to have its foundations built on cotton wool or bales of cotton, to absorb the shock waves as rail traffic crossed over the top. Improbable? Not so, according to a document written by a local man, Tommy Marsden (deceased), which is in the hands of someone known to the authors who was kind enough to allow them to see it.

The line running over the viaduct is now defunct but for a number of years before it closed it was used only when maintenance was being carried out on what is now the main East Coast Line from Newcastle upon Tyne through Durham City and on to London.

The viaduct now stands only as a proud monument to the skills of those Victorian engineers and artisans who built it.

Whether it will stand as long as the Roman Aqueduct in Spain, who can tell? We only hope some new use can be found for it in the future.

Before moving on to the third and final bridge in this trio, there is one other feature which can still be seen nestling at the foot of the column on the south side of the viaduct. This consists of a flight of steps and a landing stage which seems to lead nowhere.

In fact the steps and landing were part of Low Lambton Staithes and were used by the Victorian Ferry, a rowing boat, which carried miners between Penshaw and North Biddick Colliery.

The Footbridge

This small, narrow, steel bridge, which connects Cox Green to the north side of the river just below the Patterson Industrial Estate where once stood Low Barmston, changed the lives of those people living in the two riverside communities when it was opened in 1958. It was designed by the Chief Engineer of Durham County, Mr. G.E.Bushell.

Until that time the only way of crossing the river at this point was by rowing-boat ferry owned and operated by the Frost family, descendants of whom still live in the White House on the north side of the bridge. The ferry had, for some, been the only link to the supply of drinking water in the area.

Alice Well

Alice Well stands close to the river bank footpath in Cox Green, and until the Second World War was the community's 'tap', each family having to carry its own supply by whatever means it could.

Bricked up after water was piped into the houses, it remained that way until the 1980's when, due to public demand, it was opened up once more to allow, or so the locals say, 'the purest water for miles' to flow once more.

Note the bricked-up tunnels which come out of the hillside on the path between Cox Green and the Viaduct on the South side of the river, running through the hills to connect Lambton Sandstone Quarries, on the far side, with the river.

Here were situated the quays to which the barges came for loading to take the quarried stone down to Sunderland for loading on to larger vessels, which would transport it to its final destination anywhere in the world.

Girdle Cake Cottage

Although no longer there - more's the pity - this quaintly named dwelling, with its red tiled roof and white walls, surrounded by a small wooden fence, stood just where the Biddick Pumping Station stands today.

Here at the far end of "South View" terrace, just before you enter the wooded area of the park, you would have been able, during the 19th and early 20th centuries, indeed until the 1930's, to purchase refreshments from the cottage.

One of the specialities was "ham and egg teas" which were well sought-after by day-trippers coming up river by boat.

The Cottage's history goes back a long way but it is reputed to have been the hiding place of the Earl of Perth, James Drummond, who took refuge there after the Jacobites were defeated by the Duke of Cumberland at Culloden in 1746.

According to the story he also died there some years later, having lived in the cottage under an assumed name.

Photographs, re-produced in two books, "The River Wear" by Tyne and Wear County Council Museums (1984) and "A Message from Sunderland" by Vincent Gordon, (see list of recommended reading), show just how much the landscape has changed over the years around this stretch of the river.

The Lake at Mount Pleasant

When the planners started to develop the James Steel Park, it was decided that a small artificial lake should be included in the design, and a site was chosen.

This site was on an area of land over on the South side of the river, opposite Biddick, between the river and Mount Pleasant, which even on a map of 1988 is shown as no more than a few 'rows' of terraced houses and allotments, with what was left of Penshaw Staithes.

Some of the old houses were cleared and the site reclaimed, the lake dug and trees planted, to give what is now a pleasant picnic area.

The lake is well stocked with fish and has a large colony of ducks and other wild fowl. At least one pair of swans have made it their home and nest among the reeds and bulrushes at one end. It has a small wooden shelter at one end should the weather turn wet.
All in all a rather quiet spot, to fish or just observe the wildlife.

Worm Hill

Standing behind the "Biddick" Public House, overlooking the Fatfield Bridge, is Worm Hill.

The hill, with its war memorial on top is claimed to be "the" hill that the Lambton Worm wrapped itself around every night, after roaming the countryside, although this has been disputed by some who are more inclined to think the hill in question was Pesher (Penshaw) hill.

Different versions of the tale do give different locations, e.g., 'The Story of the Lambton Worm' by Albert L. Hind and 'The Lambton Worm' (Song) by C.M. Leumane (1867).
The choice of location is yours, after all its only a legend isn't it?

Public Houses

Within in few hundred yards of each other, close to the river bank on the north side of Fatfield Bridge, are two public houses, plus a wine bar aptly named 'The Inn Between'.

The Biddick stands at the foot of Worm Hill Terrace and is a Bass Charrington public house, which does meals and Sunday lunches throughout the year. It also has a garden to the rear.

Further along the road away from the bridge you pass what was once the Coop building, built in 1909, now a wine bar which serves pizza-style bar snacks.

Just beyond this building stands the Havelock Arms, another public house in the Vaux Breweries group, where you can obtain hot meals and bar snacks.

The Biddick Pub, Worm Hill

JAMES STEEL PARK

Distance: 5.3 klms/3.3 miles

Walking Time: 2 hours approx.

Conditions: Flat/one incline, woodland

Pathfinder: 562

Grid Ref: 312 541

Instead of parking or starting from the Biddick public house at the foot of Worm Hill Terrace, make your way across the Fatfield Bridge to the "Mount Pleasant" side of the river.

Then, leaving the bridge behind you, take the first street off on the left, which will take you down behind the row of terraced houses, the last remnants of a bygone age still standing.

At the end of the street you will find ample parking space although we would recommend that, if possible, for security's sake, but without causing an obstruction to the residents, you park in the back street itself (1).

From the street or car park walk towards the river where you will see a signpost pointing to the right saying "COX GREEN".

Following the broad tarmac path you reach a point where the river path from the bridge converges with the one you are on. Turn right at this point along the river path.

Within a few short metres a gap appears in the high hedge at the right-hand side. This is the opening on to the grassed area around the lake. This lake was created on land recovered where once Penshaw Staithes stood.

Now well stocked with fish, it is a favourite spot not only for anglers, but also for bird watchers as it is also home to a variety of wild fowl, including at least one pair of swans which nest in the bulrushes at the far end of the lake.

THE JAMES STEEL PARK.

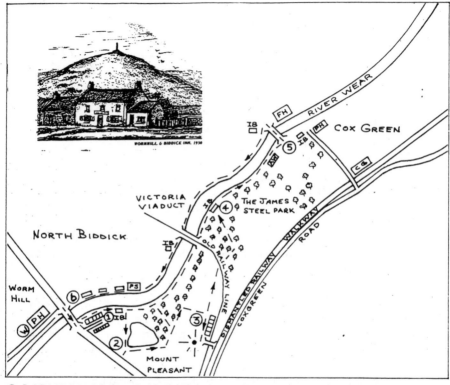

① PARKING AREA AND STARTING POINT GRID REF 312541.
② TURN LEFT AT TOP OF BANK.
③ TURN LEFT AT RAILWAY COTTAGES.
④ TURN RIGHT AT INFORMATION BOARD.
⑤ TURN LEFT OVER FOOT BRIDGE.
⑥ TURN LEFT OVER ROAD BRIDGE.
AW   ALICE WELL.
PS   PUMPING STATION ONCE WAS THE SITE OF GIRDLE
        CAKE COTTAGE.
FH   FERRY HOUSE.

You now have the decide whether to keep walking straight along the river path to "Cox Green" or try something a little more interesting.

If you decide the latter, read on.

Take an anti-clockwise route around the lake, past the little wooden shelter, and over to the path that runs down the bank towards you from the houses you can see at the top.

Then about three-quarters of the way up this incline, a path runs off to your left. A sign tells you that these woods are owned by the "Woodland Trust" and that you are welcome to walk its path (2).

The path drops slightly, so therefore remains fairly dry even in the wettest of weather.

At the end of this short section, which is through a tree-lined avenue, you reach a junction. If you turn left at this point it will put you back on the riverside path.

However you need to turn right and up the five steps which are cut into the hill side, then on to the more gently sloping incline taking you up above the River Wear.

Towards the top there is a short stretch of steep gradient, with good hard stones built into it for grip.

Next, as the path comes out of a right hand curve, there is a stile, and what should be a five-barred gate (it was missing when we made the walk!).

The stile leads into a grass field which slopes up towards a group of houses slightly to the right; these are "Railway Cottages". To the right of them is a railway bridge from the parapets of which, you can, on a clear day, see right across the countryside of this corner of the North-East of England.

Keep over to the right of the field and follow the path, which runs close to the hedge, as there is often live-stock grazing. At the top you will find the stile in the right-hand corner. Climb this on to the roadway (3).

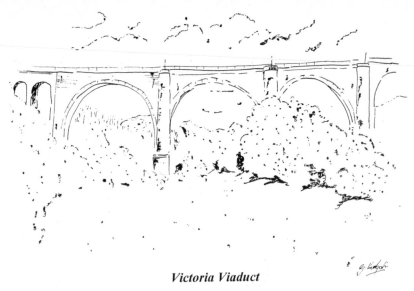

Victoria Viaduct

Turn left and walk away from the cottage towards the Victoria viaduct, the parapet railing of which you can see slightly towards your left.

The tarmac road, which is full of "pot holes", is very quiet, as it is really only used by the two farms, one half way along it, "Low Lambton", and the other at the far side of the tunnel through "Victoria Viaduct".

You will find that at a point opposite the first farm building the road divides into two, one going off to the right and the buildings, while the other, to the left, drops down an incline towards the tunnel.

Just towards the right, looking over to the farm buildings, you can just catch sight of a wooden signpost tucked in to the trees and bushes. Walking over to it, you will see that it reads "Permissible Footpath" and you can see a path running along the back of the farm building towards another tunnel.

You however will follow the broader path down and through the first tunnel.

As you are walking through it is worth reflecting how sad it is that nothing is ever recorded of the actual workmen who fitted those huge stones together. They have been long gone and forgotten, but their workmanship still stands, a monument to their skills.

A few metres (yards) through the tunnel you will see, straight ahead, the second farm, and to the left a stile and gate.

Over the stile takes you on to a soft earth path, past the Sunderland Country walk sign and into a wooded area.

At the time of our research into the walk a tree lay across the path but it could be removed at any time. There was no problem negotiating round it.

At about this point, if you look through the trees you can see the start of the viaduct proper.

The path drops towards the river until you reach a "T" junction. Once again you have the choice of turning left, which will take you straight back to the beginning of your walk, or of turning right, making your walk longer and more interesting.

Before you decide, why not scan the information board which Sunderland Council has erected at this point? (4).

You will see that by following the right-hand path, which leads to "Cox Green", there are, only a short distance along, the remains of two old tunnels, so keep a look-out for them on your right hand-side.

The path, which is firm and dry, runs slightly away from the river at this point, but there are paths running away from the main track which will take you closer if you should want to explore.

Remember, this part of the river was at one time a very busy and important industrial area for the shipment of coal and sandstone.

Right! Have you spotted the tunnels? Both have at one time been bricked up for safety, but are no longer.

These tunnels came from the Lambton Sandstone Quarries, enabling the stone to be brought right down to the river for loading onto barges, then taken down-river and put on to larger vessels for transport around the world.

We found, a few yards past the site of the first tunnel, another fallen tree, this one somewhat larger than the first, but it was possible to simply walk under it at the right-hand side; then some 100 yards on, the second tunnel entrance.

See if you can spot the stone steps buried in the undergrowth on your right. Where they lead to is anyone's guess because everything is so overgrown.

The path finally brings you to the kissing gate at the edge of "Cox Green".

Keep to the water's edge path which will allow you to see the pipe issuing water into what is called "Alice Well". This was the only source of drinking water for the communities on both sides of the river right up until the Second World War.

Turn left and cross the bridge (5) This was opened in 1958. Before which the only method of crossing was by row-boat ferry, owned by the Frost family who still live in the house on the Washington side of the bridge. So you can just imagine the problems the people on the north side had when they wanted fresh water.

At the far side of the bridge, turn left over the flat-stone path and into the car park at the left corner. The path leads out on to a large picnic area with seats and tables. Follow the path until you reach the woods at the far end, here the path rises slightly with railings on one side.

At this point the path is close to the river bank and you can see across the river to what is left of the old staithes.

Here you will find a steel five-barred gate and two steel posts set in the ground just wide enough to let a person walk through, but unfortunately mountain bikes can easily be lifted over as well so take care.

The path runs close to the river, rising and falling as it does so, through the woods. Firm underfoot, this path makes walking easy for the next quarter-mile or so.

At one point you can get a fine view of the Victoria Viaduct just before you come to the back of Victoria Bridge House, where the path deteriorates and becomes a mud bath, which never seems to dry out no matter what the season. So take care, and where possible walk along the edges for the short distance it covers.

The section you are now walking along is the ideal place in the autumn for picking black berries, rose-hips and elderberries.

The path this time passes through one of the large arches of the viaduct, giving you a close up view of this magnificent Victorian railway bridge.

At the far side is another car park with information board set in one corner.

For the sake of safety, we would not advise you to leave your car parked here at any time, but it is a good viewing-point especially if you walk down on to the grass field which stands between the river and the pathway.

Moving on, the path widens and curves for the next quarter of a mile and is used by cars and horses, so do be careful as you walk along it.

At the end of this section you come out of the woods and up to the Biddick pumping-station which stands on the site of Girdle Cake Cottage.

Girdle Cake Cottage, Biddick

Here you cross the road to the left-hand side and take the path behind the white wooden railings, as you walk past the cottages and houses that make up South View till finally you reach Fatfield Bridge (6).

Over the bridge, turn sharp left down the steps on to the little path in front of the row of terraced houses and their neat little gardens, on that side of the river.

Then at the end of the path you are back to where you started.

To conclude, there surely cannot be many walks where you can stand and admire a Victorian bridge, based on the design of a Roman aqueduct in Spain, with a copy of a Greek temple perched on a hill not a mile away.

POINTS OF INTEREST
COX GREEN/PENSHAW

Penshaw Monument

GREEKS IN BID TO PURCHASE PENSHAW
MONUMENT FOR £2.5 MILLION.

So ran the headlines of an article in the Sunderland Echo in April 1985. It went on to say that the Greek Government wanted to purchase the monument as a replacement for the original in Athens, which was so badly damaged by acid air that it was beyond repair.

If the sale went ahead, the monument was to be dismantled and 'sledged' down the hillside to Cox Green. Here it would be loaded on to barges for transporting down river, where it could be off-loaded on to a cargo boat and shipped to Greece. Once erected on the site of the old temple, a roof would be fitted to make it look like the original.

Can you imagine the outcry from the Echo's readers as they jammed the switch-board with their calls?

However the Echo did, the following day, point out the previous day's date - APRIL 1st.

The monument on top of Penshaw Hill is held dear by the people of East Durham especially those who live on Wearside, and even Tyneside.

It is a landmark, a beacon to look for as they travel up the A19 or A1M motorway, to let them know they are nearly home.

It was built by public subscription in 1844 to commemorate John Lambton (Radical Jack), First Earl of Durham and the first Governor of Canada (born 1791, died 1844).

The design was by two Newcastle architects, John and Benjamin Green, and it was built by a Sunderland firm owned by a man called Pratt. The foundation stone was laid on the 28th August 1844, the ceremony being carried out by Thomas, Earl of Zetland.

In attendance were some 400 fellow-Freemasons, Lord Lambton having been the Provincial Grand Master of the Northumberland and Durham Lodges. Over 10,000 members of the public were also reported to have witnessed the event.

The monument itself is an impressive structure and compared thus with the original:

PENSHAW	PARTHENON (ATHENS)
100 ft long x 53 ft wide	227 ft long x 101 ft wide
10 columns, 6 ft 6" diameter	54 columns, 3 ft 4" diameter
70 ft high	65 ft high

Gritstone from a quarry at Marsden and Welsh stone were used in the construction.

The word Penshaw, or Pensher as it was known, appears to be derived from the 'British' word 'Pen', meaning a hill and the Saxon 'Shaw', a wood or thicket (i.e. a wooded hill).

A photograph appeared in the Sunderland Echo on the 9th March 1973, supplied by a Mr. Matthew Murray of Philadelphia, U.S.A., showing men walking round the top of the monument. This was possible in the early days, but for safety reasons the column which has the staircase inside is now sealed up.

Some people would call it one of Britain's largest 'follies', but when, on a dark winter's night, it is fully illuminated by its floodlights, it is a beautiful and impressive structure, and one Durham people can be proud of.

The site and monument are both now in the hands of the National Trust, who manage and maintain it for the people, so that it might stand as long as the original in Athens.

Alice Well

Situated beside the river footpath at the western end of Cox Green, Alice Well is in fact a natural spring which would appear to have its source up on the hillside above the village.

The inscription above the Well states that it was rebuilt in 1855. Rebuilt from what we do not know.

It was the only supply of drinking water available to residents on both sides of the river at this point, right up until after the Second World War. This meant that until water was eventually piped into the houses all drinking water had to be collected in containers, and those living on the opposite bank had to use the rowing boat ferry belonging to the Frost family, to convey their precious liquid back to their homes.

The well fell into disuse and was bricked up, until some fifteen years ago, i.e., in 1980, it was opened up once more to allow what some of the local people consider to be the 'purest' water in the whole area to flow once more.

The Oddfellows Arms

Standing at the east end of the village of Cox Green, this small but friendly public house is owned and run by Joe and Emily Jackson. It had only recently been re-furbished when the research for this book was carried out in 1995. Although this is not a large pub by any standard, good use has been made of the space available inside, with a garden area to the rear.

One of the obvious attractions to walkers, beside the beautifully cold beer which Joe and Emily keep, must be the meals, with lunch served on Sundays throughout the year and weekdays during the summer months. Bar meals are available throughout the year. Mine hosts do advise telephoning, to ensure a place in this popular hostelry, Tel: 0191 534 6886.

The walls of the pub inside are dotted with photographs of the area in days gone by, showing how much the landscape has changed over the years. Joe and Emily are not sure just how long there has been a public house on the site, as the records only appear to go back 100 years.

There is however a strong possibility that this Cox Green hostelry could go back as far as the 17th century. Considering the history of the area and its industrial past this would not be at all surprising.

COXGREEN/PENSHAW.

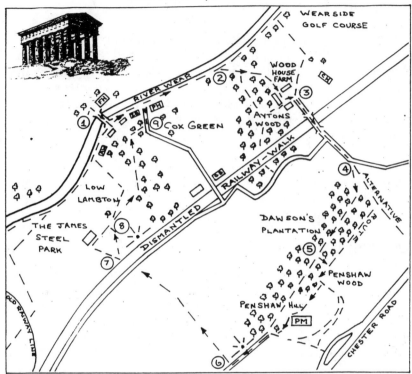

① CAR PARK GRID REF. 315541 OVER FOOTBRIDGE. TURN LEFT.
② TURN RIGHT AND UP THE STEPS INTO AYTON'S WOOD
③ TURN RIGHT FOLLOW ROAD TO FOOTBRIDGE.
④ TURN RIGHT OVER STILE.
⑤ TURN LEFT AND CLIMB STEPS, TURN RIGHT AT TOP.
⑥ TURN RIGHT, GOOD VIEW FROM HERE.
⑦ TURN RIGHT AND OVER STILE.
⑧ TURN LEFT OR RIGHT AFTER WHICH PATH YOU DECIDE ON.
⑨ TURN LEFT AND DOWN THE BANK TO ODD FELLOWS ARMS.
CS SITE OF OLD COXGREEN STATION.
PM PENSHAW MONUMENT.
CH WASHINGTON GOLF CLUB
FH FERRY HOUSE.

COX GREEN/PENSHAW

Distance: 4.67 km/2.95 miles

Walking Time: Two-and-a-quarter hours approx.

Conditions: Hilly

Pathfinder: 562

Grid Ref: 315 341

This walk is a must for those of you who have never been up to the top of Penshaw Hill but always wanted to stand under the huge stone structure of the Greek-style temple which is perched there.

It is also a must for the rest of you who have made the pilgrimage to the top via the more usual route, i.e. A19 onto the A183 Chester Road, and parked at the foot of the hill in the lay-by, because the route taken on this walk, although a less used one, is still the more interesting.

You actually start from the little car park at the North side of the footbridge into Cox Green (1). This is gained from the A1231 Sunderland to Washington turning off for Barmston, head for District 8 and follow the signpost "Wild Fowl Trust/James Steel Park" leading down to the river's edge.

For those who may have already tried the previous walk in this series (James Steel Park), you will be familiar with "Cox Green", with its mixture of houses and local pub, facing the River Wear.

So we make no excuses for bringing you through this quiet little hamlet once more, for it is in our opinion a lovely little backwater, set within easy reach of industrial Washington.

Cross the bridge into Cox Green, turn left and follow the road past the houses and village green and the "Wear Trail" Information Board, straight on past the Oddfellows Arms (which closes at 3.00 pm during the winter months).

A pair of semi-detached houses named Greenhurst stands on the right-hand side of tarmac path, while over to the river side, there are stables.

At the end of the path you reach a steel five-barred gate with a very narrow path going off to the left. This entrance did at one time have a "kissing gate" across it, but no longer.

The path should be dry to walk on at any time of the year due to the gravel chippings that have been put down, at least over the first section.

After approximately 100 yards you reach a "kissing gate" which has a "Way" sign attached, and just over this there is the River Wear trail plaque, set on a wooden plinth.

Continue from one section of woodland out into an open stretch and then, as you reach the next trees, you will find three wooden planks, crossing a stone-wall culvert (2).

A few paces after this, on the right leading up into what is Ayton's Wood, there are at first five concrete steps, followed by a very short space without steps and then a series of them to take you up the hillside.

Once up the first section, you find yourself confronted by a fork in the road. Take the right-hand route up to the point where the tree has fallen across the path. Over or round the tree you go and on to the path in front of you.

Follow this path with a fence to your left, pass the old wooden building in the field over the fence, until you at last come out into what was the stable yard of Wood House Farm, but don't worry, there is a right of way. Just remember to respect the owners' property and stick to the path as it curves over to the left around the front of the house.

Please also remember to leave the large white gates the way you find them, open or closed.

As you walk through the gates (3), turn right and up to the old railway bridge which spans what is now a country walk, but which at one time carried the Penshaw/Pallion branch line of the L & N.E.R. (London and North Eastern Railway) part of which you will recognise if you have tried Walk No. 2 in this book.

So over the bridge and up to the road as it climbs gently to the 'T' junction a little higher up.

Continue past the white buildings that stand on one corner, and on up to the first bend in the road.

It is advisable to keep well over to the right-hand side as you do so, as cars are inclined to come around the bend fairly fast, without due regard for walkers.

Just on the bend you will find a stile leading on to what is known as Grimestone Banks(4).

Take care when walking up into this field, if the weather is or has been wet, as the going can be slippery.

Once up the first incline the field develops into a more gentle slope.

You now have a choice of two routes. You can go straight over to the wire fence and stile at the foot of a steep incline, at the top of which is a path going off to the right and up to Penshaw Monument.

The second route takes you over to the edge of Dawson's Plantation, which is entered by way of a stile, and on to a National Trust permissive path through the woods.

However, before you decide, turn around, and give yourself time to admire the view, right across the Wear Valley, beyond Newcastle and on a very clear day, as far as the Cheviots.

For the purposes of this book, take the broad path as it rises and falls through the woods.

The trees are thinned out enough to allow you to spot the farm and riding stables down where Cox Green station once stood.

There are various paths going off from the main path. Ignore these until you reach one on the left, with wooden steps climbing up it (5).

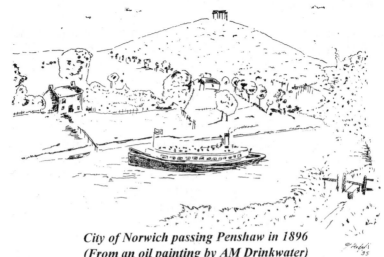

City of Norwich passing Penshaw in 1896
(From an oil painting by AM Drinkwater)

At this point you once again have a choice of routes. Up the steps will bring you within walking distance of the Monument, while the lower, broad path skirts around the hill, missing out the final climb and the Monument.

So up the steps, and you find yourself in the corner of a field and on the path which came along the top of the woods.

Walking diagonally across the field, you reach a broad cart track. Simply follow this up to the Monument.

See if you can spot the column which holds the stairs to the roof once you reach the monument itself.

Once again take a good look all around. The river is magnificent, and you can see how this part of the Wear Valley cuts a green swathe through housing estates and factory sites of the Washington district.

Weather permitting, this is good spot to take a break before starting your descent back down to Cox Green.

You pick up the path, which is to your right if you stand with your back to the plinth which holds the details of the Monument on it.

It is in fact a series of steps leading down to a path which runs alongside a wire fence. This leads on to a further set of steps at the foot of which stands a stile.

Head straight down the broad path passing, at the top, on the right, a gate which leads into the woods.

This is in fact the end of the path through the woods, which you can take if you prefer not to climb up to the Monument.

Walking down the lane between the hedgerows, you pass the first gate on the right and continue down to where you will find a stile (6). The lane leads to Middle Barmwell Farm.

Climb the stile and descend down through the fields, keeping to the path close to the left-hand hedge, to Cox Green Road.

Cross this with care, and walk over and across the old railway track in the direction of "Penshaw North House Farm". Cross this with care, and walk over and across the old railway track in the direction of Penshaw North House Farm. There is, on a wooden gate-post at the right of the path, a Way sign pointing over to the right.

But to find the path, walk past the sign and hedges, and here you will find a stile (7), but climb this with care as a log in front of it slopes sharply into the field.

Walk through the field, keeping to the right, as the field can be muddy after wet weather.

In the far corner there is a kissing gate with a Way sign attached.

This leads into what appears to be a farm yard 'dump', which we found to be very muddy in wet weather.

Cross diagonally over to the right-hand corner here. Past the large tree on your left you will see a broad path going off into a field, while to the right of this stands a stile with a Way sign attached (8).

The broader path curves round to the left and descends through the next field and on to a wooden stile. Over this and you are on a large step that brings you on to the river path.

Turn right, and it is only a short walk to the kissing gate at the edge of Cox Green.

The broad path runs in front of a large house which has, hanging from its gate, a large "Private" notice. Worry not, it is a public right of way.

From here you can see Cox Green bridge.

Take the path close to the river and you will pass what was Cox Green's only supply of drinking water until after the Second World War, Alice Well.

Now back to the farm dump and the other path (8).

This one runs down the east side of Cox Green Gill, while the other runs down the west side.

It also runs through woodlands eventually coming out on a bend in the road (9) leading down to the Oddfellows Arms in Cox Green.

We leave the decision entirely up to you as to which route you take.

No matter which you take, we are sure you will have enjoyed an exhilarating walk up to Penshaw Monument.

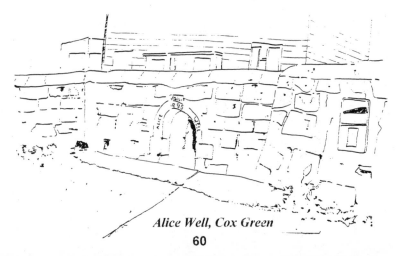

Alice Well, Cox Green

POINTS OF INTEREST
LUMLEY CASTLE

Lumley Castle

The Castle provides the magnificent backdrop to the new Durham County Council Club Ground and Sports Centre, along the banks of the River Wear and Chester-le-Street. It was built by Sir Ralph Lumley in the 14th century, pre-dating its neighbour Lambton Castle by some 500 years.

Now a residential hotel with 62 individually designed bedrooms, it is noted for its award-winning Elizabethan Banquets, which are held throughout the year. It is also a very popular venue for weddings.

It is haunted - and what castle is not haunted? - by a white lady by the name of Lily of Lumley.

The silhouette of the castle was used as a trademark for the bricks produced at Lumley Brick Works, which is said to have produced over a million bricks with the castle stamped on each one.

A second connection between the Castle and the brickworks is that by tradition the manager of the works was granted the right to live in Ford Cottage, on the Lumley Estate.

Half-Penny Bridge

This bridge was built to provide the estate workers with easier access to Chester-le-Street. Lord Scarborough provided the capital to build the pedestrian crossing, which he opened in 1898.

A charge of 1/2p (old coinage) was levied to help pay back his lordship's investment.

It was finally bought by the then Urban Council in 1950 for the sum of £200, only to be demolished 14 years later, after a cantilever footpath was added to Lumley New Bridge, which had been built by J.C. Renwick in 1914 at a cost of £17,600 as well as an unknown sum to compensate the Earl of Scarborough for loss of toll earnings.

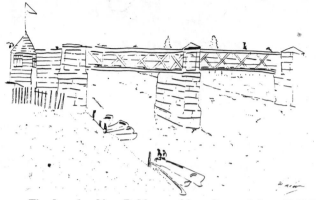

The Lumley New Bridge and boat house (circa 1930/40)

This bridge, which crosses the river between Ropery Lane and Lumley New Road, is itself to be replaced at some time, hopefully in 1996, by a new bridge. as the 80-year-old structure is now badly in need of major repairs and not really suitable for the amount of vehicular traffic that passes over it daily.

The "Hags"

Trying to trace place names can sometimes be very frustrating, as there seems to be no rhyme or reason as to why a place has a particular name, and this seems to be the case with a section of land which lies between Lumley Castle and the A1 motorway, "The Hags".

Depending on how you pronounce the word, and here again the author found even local people unsure, the most popular seemed to be "Hags", as in "bags".

If this is correct, then two possible explanations come to mind. The first: Hag "defined as an old dame or witch". The second and more likely is in the New English Dictionary (1932 edition), which defines "hags" as "tufty hillocks of firmer ground in a bog".

Continuing along this line of reasoning, the piece of land over towards the river Wear is called "The Haughs", which is defined as "Low-lying land close to a river".

So, having given our explanation of this particular mystery, we move on to another.

Virgin Well

This is shown on maps of the area to lie between "the Cottages" and Lumley Lodge on the east side of the A1M motorway.

No evidence of a well of any type can be found, and although it is on an Ordnance Survey map of 1898, local historians are unable to supply a positive explanation of how the name came about.

One theory has it, that it is not, nor ever was, a "Well", but an air shaft from one of the local coal mines, possibly 9th Pit, which was located next to White House, which stands on the right-hand side of the A183 out of Chester-le-Street, just up in the hill from the site.

Relay Station

No mystery surrounds this building close to the Cottages, which has all the antennae sticking out of it. This is one of Cellnet's (Radio Phones) relay stations.

Lumley Lodge

This of course is the original gate-house to the Lumley Estate, functioning until the A1M motorway sliced through the grounds.

Chester-le-Street Park

The original riverside park, which at the time of writing is being redeveloped as part of the "New Riverside Complex", was first suggested in July 1917.

This was to be the town's memorial to the local men who had lost their lives in the Great War (1914-1918).

For various reasons it did not get under way until the 1930's, and only after a by-pass had been built around the town, this being what is still known as the old A1 trunk road.

It was finally completed and opened to the public in 1934, a park with bandstand, bowling green, play and picnic areas, to be enjoyed by all the family.

Changing patterns of leisure have meant that the park and riverside needed to be re-developed along with car parking spaces.

So a slightly smaller park is being prepared, allowing excess land to be made into car parks, and will hopefully be completed by the end of 1996.

Cricket Ground and Sports Complex

What can one say about the County Ground (opened 1995) except that it must surely rate as one of the finest in the country, with all its facilities and the backdrop of Lumley Castle, while the rest of the complex can only enhance the area and provide a wide spectrum of sporting venues for national and international events.

Nature Reserve

Although still in the early stages of development at the time of writing this book, the "Reserve", set on the loop of the river, down from the complex, will, we are sure, be a huge success as it matures over the years, as well as being an added attraction for walkers who enjoy the delights of the riverside and the wildlife which will make its home there.

The Boathouse, Lambton Estate

Marina, Sunderland

Victoria Viaduct

I

View from Victoria Viaduct, looking west

Old workings, Lampton sandstone quarry

Biddick Bridge

The Biddick pub from Biddick Bridge

Old railway bridge, now foot bridge, between Rainton Park wood and East Moor Leazes

Elvert Bridge, Durham City (taken from Feardon Walk)

IV

LUMLEY CASTLE

Distance: 4.19 km/2.6 miles

Walking Time: One and three-quarter hours approx.

Conditions: Flat riverside/hilly

Pathfinder: 562

Grid Ref: 582 509

You start this walk from any one of the car parks close to the County Cricket Ground on the Chester-le-Street side of the River Wear. From here you walk over the bridge in the direction of Lumley Castle.

Keeping to the left-hand side of the bridge as you do so, look for the "Footpath" signpost, indicating the path going off to the left, just as you reach the far side of the river. This is a typical riverside path, which changes in underfoot conditions depending on the weather.

As you walk along, you will notice a large concrete block set on the river bank. This was the foundation block for the 1/2p (old coinage) bridge.

A short stroll from this point brings you to the fence which surrounds Lumley Boat House, and the path that runs up the outside of the garden. This is only a narrow path which can change from dust-dry to ankle deep mud depending on the weather, so care is needed sometimes when negotiating this short section.

Past this, the path opens up into a wider, firmer track, which is the roadway into the Boat House and gardens.

You will then find yourself walking up a slight slope in the direction of Lumley Castle and through the Golf Course. (IT IS A PUBLIC FOOTPATH, WITH RIGHT OF WAY.)

Over to the left a steel bridge spans Lumley Park Burn. You will see that this has a steel gate barring the way to the general public.

LUMLEY CASTLE

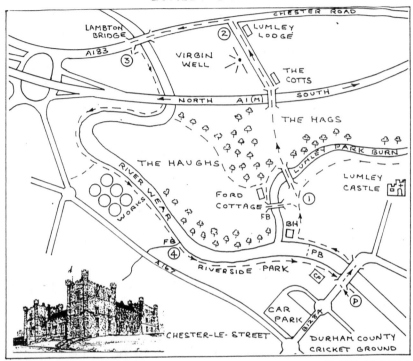

℗ PARKING AREA NEXT TO SPORTS CENTRE GRID REF 284508
① TURN LEFT OVER HAGS BRIDG BRIDGE AND STRAIGHT ON.
② TURN LEFT AT END OF LANE.
③ OVER ROAD BRIDGE TURN LEFT AND DOWN THE STEPS TO
   RIVER SIDE PATH.
④ STRAIGHT OVER FOOT BRIDGE FOLLOWING RIVERSIDE PATH.
PB SITE OF HALF PENNY BRIDGE.
CP CHILDREN'S PLAY AREA.

So climb further up the gravel path, until you are level with the little stone bridge over to your left. Once level with this bridge walk across the grass towards it (1). You are then walking across the 10th green of the golf course.

Don't worry, this is a public footpath, but while walkers have the right of way, please spare a thought for the golfers who may be just about to tee off. (It costs nothing to be courteous and polite and goes a long way to creating good feelings.)

This is Hags Bridge, which is made of stone though in need of repair, as only one side, the left, has a parapet.

See if you can see the surveyor's "bench mark", which is cut into the stone. This symbol is used to determine height above sea-level when maps are drawn.

Once across the bridge, keep over to the right-hand side of the path and walk up towards the stile at the top.

A word of warning at this point. This is another section which deteriorates into a mud bath after wet weather, and keeping to the grass sides may not help as the ground under the grass can still be very slippery.

Just before reaching the stile, a path leading off to the right and into the woods is one you come across in the Chester-le-Street/ Lumley walk in this book.

Over the stile and you are on the Hags, where, if you are quiet and it is the right time of year, you will see a good number of pheasants walking around.

The ground rises steeply at first towards the trees on the ridge, and then more gently to the far corner of the field at the footbridge across the A1M motorway.

Unfortunately, this bridge is approached over muddy ground, obviously churned up by cattle, through a five-barred and kissing gate all marked with Way signs (yellow arrow, on a green background).

Through these and you are on a dry tarmac path leading on to the bridge proper where, even on a calm day, it is wise to hang on to any headgear you may be wearing, as the traffic rushes below causing an up-draught.
How many times have you passed under this bridge driving down the A1M, and never given it a second glance?

At the far side stand two semi-detached cottages which don't appear to bear names and only appear on a 1979 (amended 1981) map of the area as the "Cotts" or Cottages.

These would have housed staff of the Lumley Estate at one time. They stand on what was once a roadway into the estate, as can be seen at the other end of this broad path where a pair of large wrought-iron gates stands, and of course the lodge (Lumley Lodge by name), stranded now between the A1M and Chester Road A183.

However before you reach the Lodge, you pass on the right the Cellnet mobile telephone relay station and then another. Approximately 200 yards over the hedge to the left is the site of "Virgin Well", now only two words on a map.

As you pass through the gates you will find yourself on the verge of the busy Chester Road (A183). You need to cross at this point as the pavement is on the far side(2). Be warned, the road has a long curve in it and the traffic is very fast and heavy.

Cross the road and turn down the hill on to Lambton Bridge, where once again you need to be on the other side.

Once there, walk to the far end of the bridge and here you will find a series of steps leading down to the river's edge under the bridge and on to a narrow path (3).

Turn right and follow this, with the field to your right and the river to the left.

The path is dry and even, making it easy to walk along, passing as it does under the concrete structure of the A1M motorway bridge over the River Wear at this point.

There is little that can be said about the architecture of a bridge of this type, unlike those built by past generations of engineers, except to say that it is functional, and has large areas of flat surfaces on which the graffiti 'artists' can execute their works of art.

Keep following the path, which remains close to the river's edge, until you find yourself in a green field.

On a fine day this can be an ideal spot to take a break. Alternatively you can continue past the steel fencing which surrounds Chester-le-Street's treatment works, down to the left and across a small steel footbridge which spans Chester Burn, which runs into the river at this point.

Here you will probably find a host of mallard ducks which gather in the hope of being fed by the people who pass by.
At the far side of this bridge, you can drop down to the water's edge along the concrete path (4).

With luck you may find the odd seat still not vandalised (the Council do try to replace and repair as often as possible) where you can sit, have a break and watch the river go by.

From this point the path was, at the time of our research, flooded, and it was necessary to climb up on to the grass embankment.

However, at most times of the year it is possible to continue along the river path into the play area, which is equipped for younger children. There is also a toilet block at the edge of the area.
Walking along through the play area, and looking across the river, you can see first of all Ford Cottage, and then, close the river's edge, the Boat House, which you passed on that section of the walk.

Reaching the end of this part of the walk, you have two choices. You can walk up the grass embankment and on to the road, which you may need to cross depending on the point from which you started the walk.

However, if you still have time in hand, why not continue along the river bank at the far side of the road via the subway? This will give you the opportunity to have a look at the County Cricket ground and the rest of the Sports Complex, or even take in the wildlife nature reserve just beyond.

Even if you do not, we hope you have enjoyed the rest of the walk and will try some of the others in this book.

POINTS OF INTEREST
CHESTER-LE-STREET / CASTLE DENE

Great Lumley

Great Lumley sits high on the hills to the East of Chester-le-Street, separated from it by the River Wear, and unlike so many semi-isolated villages which grew up around the local coal-mine, was in fact a settlement of some stature before the Norman Conquest in 1066.

Said to be one of the only Saxon villages to have held out against William the Conqueror's armies, it only finally came to heel under the rule of the Prince Bishops, appointed by William I.

Through its long and turbulent history, the people of Lumley remained very independent of their neighbours down the hill and across the river (Chester-le-Street).

Only a rowing-boat ferry connected the two communities up until 1898, when the Earl of Scarborough built a pedestrian bridge across the river.

Vehicular traffic had to wait another 16 years before a wider crossing (Lumley New Bridge) was constructed. By this time the Durham coalfield had spread, and Lumley had its own pit (Lumley 6th), as well as a large stone quarry.

Both of these have now gone and the village has very little to offer in the way of employment. It now attracts people who wish to live away from, but commute to the larger towns in the area, for work.

The Warriors Arms

This pub was known at one time as the Lumley Castle, and stands close to the edge of the village. In it you will find the locals only too willing to talk about themselves and their village.

Around the walls of the bar hang numerous old local photographs, as well as a map of the district dated 1896. This map shows just how remote the village was even at the end of the 19th century. At the same time it shows how this small community supported up to

11 public houses, Alms Houses (shown on the map as a hospital), a church and chapel dating back to 1710. The chapel can be seen standing on the left hand side of Back Lane, which is the road leading into Lumley from the river. Partly converted into a private dwelling, it is still awaiting completion.

The 'Bloody' Tree

Across the road from where the school house stood, a signpost points towards a barred gate. This leads onto Old Mill Lane, where, history has it, a young girl named Anne Walker met a gruesome death in 1631 at the hands of two local men who were accused and found guilty on the evidence of her ghost.

The old oak tree, which is approximately a quarter of a mile down the lane, and known as "The Bloody Tree", is said to mark the place where Anne met her untimely death.

The full story appeared in the "Washington Post" on the 13th February 1994, and is taken from a Sunderland Echo publication entitled "Crimes of Yesteryear", still available in local book stores in the North East of England.

Garden House

With what is left of its walled gardens, Garden House lies in the heart of Lumley Park Wood, across the burn behind "Lumley Castle".

It was built sometime in the 18th century along with Ford Cottage and the Boat House, according to Mr. Richards of Chester-le-Street, who actually lived in Garden House for a number of years.

The "House" would have been home to the head gardener of the estate. The gardens would have supplied the castle kitchens with almost all they needed in the way of vegetables, while such fruits as grapes, peaches and of course tomatoes would have all come from the large greenhouse which stood on the south-facing wall in the garden area.

This would have been heated in the colder months of the year by a system of hot pipes fed by water from a large boiler.

Over the years, as the castle's dependence on its own supplies of fruit and vegetables waned, the garden fell into disrepair and it now lies derelict.

The house however is still occupied, the present family having lived there for some 15 years (1980), and it is interesting that the head of the house actually worked as a game warden on the neighbouring Lambton Estate, in what was the "Lambton Safari Park" until it closed down some years ago.

Ford Cottage

Ford Cottage has already been mentioned in the Lumley Castle walk in this book (No. 6).

The Boat House

Built at about the same time, this was the ferryman's home until the building of the half-penny bridge.

Refreshments

The Warriors Arms, which is tenant-owned, supplies meals on Saturday evening and Sunday lunchtime only, but the owners are intending to extend these facilities sometime in the future. A range of beers and lagers are available to help quench the thirst of walkers on a warm day.

The Dog and Gun is another public house, which stands on the same side of the road as the Warriors Arms. It too serves hot meals and bar snacks. The choice is yours.

CHESTER-LE-STREET / CASTLE DENE

Distance: 7.6 km

Walking Time: Two and three-quarter hours

Conditions: Gentle slopes and hilly woodland paths

Pathfinder: 562/572

Grid Ref: 582 509

You start this walk on the east side of Lumley New Bridge which spans the river close to Lumley Castle.

There are ample car parks on the Chester-le-Street side of the river, but in the summer months these are likely to be filled by cricket fans, so it would be best to tackle the walk either when the Durham team are playing away or at a time of the year when no cricket is played at all.

If you stand on the far side of the bridge, facing the castle, you will see, over to the right, a public footpath notice.

Go down the steps, and simply follow the path. The river will be on your right and the B1284 on your left.

The path is firm and provides good all weather walking, with a chance of catching a glimpse of the odd pheasant.

At the far end of this section, the path starts to rise, and here, after wet weather, it can be muddy, which is where a walking stick comes in handy.

The path reaches a stile and then passes between two barred gates, which close off a private road to the pumping station down to your right.
Cross the road between the gates to the second stile.

Over this and the path climbs up to the right and into a wooded section, two oaks standing by the side of the path.

CHESTER-LE-STREET / CASTLE DENE

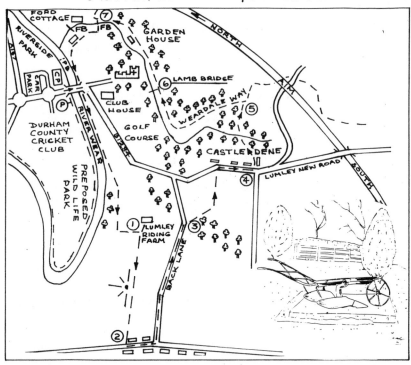

ⓅCAR PARK GRID REF. 284 508.
① TURN RIGHT.
② TURN LEFT.
③ TURN RIGHT.
④ TURN LEFT AND DOWN THE LANE.
⑤ TURN LEFT.
⑥ STRAIGHT ON AT LAMB BRIDGE.
⑦ TURN LEFT OVER FOOTBRIDGE THEN TURN RIGHT.

This climb also can be muddy but if it is, try walking up on the grass sides, if you are to negotiate it with dry boots.

As you come out on to a open field look back towards the river, and there at the bottom of the incline is the water pumping station, while across the river and to the right stands the Sports Complex.

From the edge of the field, follow the path round to the right until you reach the corner where the woods and fields meet. Then veering around to the left, keeping the hedge to your right hand, walk up the field in the direction of the group of buildings at the top, this being Lumley Riding Farm.

In the top corner of the field, you will find a stile to climb, before turning right, and after a few more yards, yet another one with a steel gate at right angles to it.

Over this and you are on the path to Great Lumley.

The view from this spot is really lovely (1). On a clear day you can see right across the rural countryside of Durham on your left, sweeping past Chester-le-Street to your right, and on to Newcastle in the far distance.

It can only be said that this view even improves as the path takes you up the hillside towards Great Lumley itself. The walking is firm, and the path remains dry for the next quarter of a mile or so.

Then, as you top the crest of the hill Great Lumley lies to the left, while to your right, down in the valley, you can see the big loop in the River Wear and the finger of land at the head of the Sports Complex, which is to become a wildlife area of some 12 hectares (30 acres) when completed, hopefully by the year 2000.

Walk diagonally towards the left and the Public Footpath signpost, behind what was the School House, now a private dwelling.

The path actually runs behind the building, but to the right there is a small patch of grassed-over land. Walking over this and down on to the road at the front of School House gives you the opportunity to take a rest on the seat opposite (2).

Behind the seat lies a broad path which takes you past the "Bloody Tree" (see Local Interest Section). To see what is left of the tree entails a walk of approximately a quarter of a mile there and back.

Setting off again from the seat, you head in the direction of Great Lumley passing farms on your right which have old ploughshares in their front gardens, giving a nice rural touch to this pleasant corner of the village.

As you come level with the bungalow, called (what else?) Castle View, turn left and walk down the road called Back Lane, in the direction of Lumley Castle, passing the allotments on your left as you do so.

The broad tarmac pavement takes you down the hill in an easy descent, passing the more modern housing of Lumley over to the right, while to your left is Riding Hill Cottage. The roadway is to "Lumley Riding Farm".

Just a few yards beyond this, over to the right-hand side of the road, you will see a footpath going off across between two fields (3).

Cross the road at this point, but do so with care, as the traffic travels at speed along this stretch.

Once safely across, simply follow the path. Ignoring the one off to the right which enters a wooded stretch.

Towards its end, this path bears to the left and comes out on to Lumley New Road.

This road needs to be crossed, and as with the previous one this should be done with care.

When you reach the other side, turn right and follow the pavement up past the aged miners' cottages and terraced houses of Tinckler Terrace (4).

At the end of the terrace turn left in the direction of the allotments and garages, which are set on either side of the broad path.

Just beyond the garages a public footpath sign stands pointing straight ahead.

At the end of this path a stile takes you on to a path leading into Castle Dene. Follow the path as it curves to the left and down to the crossing over the burn which runs through a tunnel at this point.

Then the path climbs up the other side of the Dene, which can be muddy during or after wet weather, so take care.

At the top of the climb a path runs across in front of you (5). Turn left at this point and simply follow the path as it wanders through the woods, until you reach a point where it starts to descend rather steeply, and the path is very uneven. Once you reach the bottom a broad path cuts across the one you are on, and to your left is a small stone bridge crossing the burn, Lamb Bridge (6).

Continue along the path, to the right, away from the bridge. This will bring you to an old brick wall, with a large sign telling you to "Beware of the dogs", but don't be put off by this, or by the fact that you appear to be walking into some-one's garden, which you are.

The high wall surrounds what were once the vegetable gardens belonging to the Castle, now derelict, leaving only the name of the house, Garden House, to give any indication as to its past history.

The dogs belong to the present tenants, and while the guard dog is kept locked up during the day, the other wanders the yard, barking rather loudly, but is no threat to you.

Following the path, you will see the "Right of Way" signs on the gate post. Open the gate and walk into the yard. Please remember to close the gate again once you are through.

Cross the yard and keep over to the right of the house where you will find a small wooden gate, which also needs to be kept closed.

Go through the gate and down the path back into the woods as it follows the banks of the Burn. You will find most of this section dry and easy to follow.

Before you reach the next incline, there is a small culvert which runs down into the burn, crossed by two planks of wood which have been lain across.

As the path comes to the top of the incline and the edge of the woods, a broad path runs across it.

Here you will see numerous Way signs pointing in all directions. You need to follow the one pointing to the left down the hill towards the stone bridge (7).

This path can be very muddy depending on the time of year you make the walk.

As you cross the bridge, see if you can spot the surveyor's bench mark cut in the stone-work.

Across the bridge and you are on the 10th green of Lumley Golf Club; don't worry, there is a public right of way across the green, but do please give a thought for any golfers who may be about to tee off.

Walk across the green to the gravel path by the shortest possible route.

Once on the gravel path, turn right and follow it down the hill, passing Ford Cottage, which sits on the hill amongst the trees at the far side of the burn.

Continue on to the earth path when the gravel runs out, down and over to the left, where there is a Public Footpath sign pointing in the direction of the River Wear.

The path goes between the golf course on the left and a hedge on the right, which runs around the Boat House.

In bad weather this is another section which becomes muddy and water-logged, but does dry out at other times. Unfortunately it cannot be avoided.

You simply have to wade in and follow it to where it veers left alongside the river bank, which is usually dry.

A few yards after leaving the Boat House path you can see a concrete block set into the river bank.

This was the support for what was the first crossing of the Wear at this point, Lord Scarborough's half-Penny Bridge, the first "dry" link between Chester-le-Street and Lumley.

All you need to do now is stroll back to Lumley New Bridge from where you started the walk, which we hope you have enjoyed.

Finchale Priory

If you are visiting Finchale Priory ('Finkle' to North-Easterners), (now managed by the National Trust) for the first time, or even if you are more regular visitor, you cannot fail to see why the monks of Durham chose to build a priory there. What they sought was remoteness and tranquillity. Today the remoteness has partly gone, but the tranquillity can still be found.

Saint Godric

The priory was built in memory of Saint Godric and dedicated to John the Baptist. Godric came to the area in 1110 A.D. after a vision of St. Cuthbert told him to take up his abode at Finchale.

Godric's original dwelling was approximately a mile upstream from where the priory stands, and was little more than a cave infested with poisonous snakes and adders as well as wolves.

Taken by his piety - it is said he plunged his body into the icy waters of the river at sunset and prayed until sunrise - his followers built first a wooden and then a stone chapel at his hermitage.

The priory was intended as a retreat for the monks of Durham Cathedral, but sadly was never completed in the manner they had intended.

It finally fell into decay after Henry VIII's dissolution of the monasteries in 1536 A.D. in his attempt to curb the power of the churches and their strong connections with the Vatican.

Godric's remains were buried in a stone coffin in the choir of the later monastic church.

A booklet called "The Tragedy of Finchale Priory" which deals in some depth with St. Godric's life at Finchale, can be obtained for a modest sum, on the site, along with other booklets of local interest.

The Farm

The farm dates back to the time of the building of the priory in the 13th century, and was purchased by the present owners, the Welsh family, from the Dean and Chapter of Durham on the 13th May 1951.

Included in the sale was a small caravan site, which Mr. and Mrs. Welsh have greatly expanded and improved over the years, so that now, along with the larger residential caravans, there exist room and full amenities for casual or towing vans.

The owners' policy over the years has been to encourage families on to the site, which has proved to be a popular move and one that leads to a more enjoyable holiday.

The Shop which is attached to the farm house sells sweets, ice-cream, etc., as well as postcards and literature giving details about the priory.

It is here that you can obtain permission to use the alternative route which we have marked out. This can be done at the same time as you pay the 50p parking fee, if you have come by car.

The fee, which we have been assured by the owners will not be going up in the foreseeable future, is well worth paying, so that you know your car is in safe hands.

Next to the shop stands an old-fashioned red telephone box, in working order, for public use.

We have not included the opening times or entrance fees for the priory ruins, as they can change from time to time, but they are displayed at the entrance to the site.

For those who like to trace the origins of place names, the word Finchale is derived from two words, "Finch" and "hale", "hale" being another word for "haugh", a flat area of land close to a river, and "finch" as in the bird, probably the chaffinch.

So it has become the place of the finches.

FINCHALE PIORY

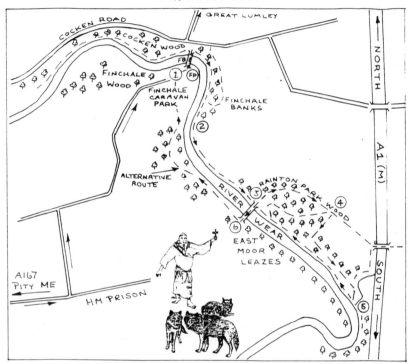

① CAR PARK AND STARTING POINT GRID REF. 297472 OVER
   FOOTBRIDGE TURN RIGHT.
② FOLLOW TRACK ALONG RIVER BANK (TAKE CARE)
③ TURN LEFT UP STEPS INTO RAINTON PARK WOODS /
   MOORHOUSE WOODS.
④ TURN RIGHT.
⑤ TURN RIGHT AND FOLLOW RIVERSIDE PATH.
⑥ TURN RIGHT.

FINCHALE PRIORY

Distance:	4.97 km/3.08 miles
Walking Time:	Two hours approx.
Conditions:	Flat/steps and inclines
Pathfinder:	572
Grid Ref:	297 472

Sometimes it is difficult to decide which of two routes you should take on a particular walk, as is the case with the one from Finchale Priory.

In this particular case there is, at the beginning of the walk on the South side of the river, a short section of 150 yards or so which needs to be negotiated with care, as you climb over tree roots along the river bank, and even this is only possible in drier weather, when the river is not in flood.

Then there is an alternative route, for which permission must be obtained from the farm house shop; this is essential (1).

Both routes do end up at the same point at about one-third of the way through the walk, and both have their own attractions.

So, let's start with the route along the South side which will be reached by crossing the wooden bridge beside the farm house after parking your car (payment at the shop).

Turn right down the stairs at the far side of the bridge, keeping the river to your right, and walk along the path through the wooded area opposite the priory, for as far as you can go. That is until you reach the wire fence around a grass field (2).

It is at this point that you need to get right down to the river's edge, as there is no real footpath around the field, and you are not allowed to walk through it either.

So, dropping down to the water's edge, make your way carefully along the bank picking your way over and around the tree roots, until you can climb back up the bank at the far end of the field, some 200 yards.

From here, the walk is straightforward with a good firm path passing through un-tended ground and then alongside a cultivated field, before entering into a woodland area.

Here the path rises slightly for a few yards, before dropping down to a small, easily crossed culvert which runs down from the hillside into the Wear.

Just over this stream the path rises up to the left, before coming out at the end of a small steel bridge which spans the river at this point.

You will see next to the bridge a signpost stating that this is "National Trust Property Moorhouse Woods" although the ordnance survey maps show it as "Raintonpark Wood". Just why the Trust have called it one name and the map producers another, we are unable to find out (3).

However, no matter, it is up into these woods that you will go.

At this point we would like to guide you to the same spot via the alternative route.

Once again, from the car park at the Priory (not forgetting to pay your fee), you can, while at the shop, ask permission to use the path through the caravan site (show them this book).

The owners have assured us that as long as permission is requested, there should be no problem, but do remember it is still the owners right to refuse.

Once permission has been given, turn back to the car park, then, turning left, with the Priory on your left, walk up the broad path to the caravan park on the hillside.

Follow the path as it passes between the caravans and past the tubular barrier next to the toilet and shower block.

Then just beyond this the tarmac track ends, and from now on it is a cart track, which after rain can be muddy.

Passing over the stile at the barred gate, you now enter a wooded area above the river.

The path is easy to follow with no diversions as it rises and falls throughout this section.

You then find yourself out in an open grass field, walk straight across this to the woods at the far side.

Reaching these woods leaves you with only a short walk, and a small culvert to cross before you are on the steel footbridge.

See if you can spot the ruins of an old war-time bunker in the undergrowth, over to the left, just before you reach the bridge.

Across the bridge and you have reached the spot where these two routes converge, at the base of the steps climbing up into Moorhouse Woods. From here it is a circular route through the woods and back down alongside the river.

Taking the path up into the woods themselves, prepare yourself for a fairly steep climb, which is eased by the steps cut by the National Trust (3).

Trees such as spruce, oak, pine and ash grow in abundance throughout the whole area, and in spring or summer the ground is carpeted with woodland flowers.

The trees, which are well spaced out, give an air of freedom as you follow the path through the woods, until finally you reach a corner where the woods meet a large green field.

Here you follow this around to the right, with the stone wall to your left hand, until you reach the far end of the field and a "T" junction (4); turn right and walk on until you can see the river below you, through the trees.

This is an ideal spot to take a well-earned breather, using one of the fallen trees as a seat, and admire the view through the trees, of the valley and river below.

See if, when you are sitting there, you can spot the tree which has two trunks, but whose branches have grown out and "fused" together.

Once you have rested, it is now time to wind your way down the steep incline to the valley floor.

There are steps cut into the hillside, which make the going easier, but take care, because the bank to the left drops steeply to a burn that runs down to the river, and the steps can be very slippery after wet weather.

At the foot of the steps you will find yourself alongside the burn. Take a look at the floor and sides, see how it has been inlaid with stone slabs and a wall built up (5), for what purpose we are unsure, perhaps it was a source of drinking water at one time.

Turn to your right and away from the burn, keeping the river to your left hand.

You could if you wanted turn left at the foot of the steps and follow the path in that direction, but unfortunately it only comes to a "dead end" and you then have to retrace your steps.

So follow the path downstream, through the woods, with the old quarry cliffs towering up on your right.

The path is firm, dry and very flat, indeed ideal walking conditions.

Watch out for the mallards, which seem to breed in large numbers along this stretch of the river.

Deer roam the woods and hillside in this area, and have been photographed by the authors during their research for this book. So keep your eyes and ears open, who knows?

All too soon you find yourself back at the steel footbridge, and the decision has to be made as to which route you will take back to the Priory (6).

Please remember that even if you did not use the alternative route through the caravan park on the way out, but intend to return by it, obtain permission from the shop.

Should you not comply with the owners instructions, it will only cause problems for other walkers.

Which ever one you do choose, we are sure you will enjoy the walk. No matter which season in the year you choose to make your visit, we know you will not be disappointed by the scenery.

However, if you want to feel the tranquillity that those monks of long ago felt, try visiting the site and carrying out the walks in the autumn (October/November), when there are fewer visitors around.

This is the time when the trees in the woods and slopes above Finchale are about to shed their leaves, and those beautiful autumn colours can be seen, ranging from reds, through the hues of brown to yellow, a sight no one should miss.

What adult, let alone child, can resist kicking their feet through the carpets of leaves already covering the paths.

Once back at the Priory, if you still have time to spare, why not purchase one of the splendid little books about Finchale Priory from the shop and have a look around the site to finish off what we hope has been a enjoyable day around the Finchale Priory walks.

The farmhouse and priory ruins, Finchale

87

Moorhouse Estate

When Edward Fenwick Boyd bought himself some land at Moorhouse, West Rainton, in 1856, there was already a small hamlet of about 10 houses established there.

Edward Fenwick Boyd had been a mining engineer, a founder member and second president of the North of England Institute of Mining and Mechanical Engineers, which was established in 1852.

Then in 1871 he was instrumental in the founding at Newcastle College, which was affiliated to Durham University, the Mining College.

He had four children, two of whom followed their father's profession as mining engineers.

Of these, Robert married Annie Matthews of Brentwood in Essex in 1887. They had two children, and one of these, Edward, had the unhappy record of being one of the first fatalities of the Great War of 1914-1918. He was killed, aged 24 years, on 20th September 1914.

His father Robert died as a result of a riding accident. A fall from his horse affected his eyesight and he died a few weeks later in the south of England.

The house and estate in Durham suffered to a degree until they were purchased from the heirs and successors of the Boyd family in 1939 by the Durham County Orthopaedic Association, with a view to building a hospital for disabled people.

The second World War (1939-45) put paid to this scheme, and when in 1948 the National Health Service took over the aims and principles of the association, it was decided that the premises close to Finchale Abbey, purchased in the early 1940's were big enough.

It was not until 1965 that the Durham County Scout Association bought the estate, the ruined house and 13 acres of land.

Scouting Activities Centre

It took five more, long and hard years before the centre was officially opened in 1970.

The site was cleared and levelled to allow the building of the accommodation which provides for parties of up to 40 people on double bunk beds in six dormitories. Two separate sets of showers, toilets and wash basins make it suitable for mixed parties.

A large main hall allows for indoor activities and facilities, with two further sets of toilets downstairs. The kitchen is fully equipped to cater for up to 40 people, and adjacent is the dining room, with connecting serving hatch. A furnished lounge is available for Leaders and adults or may be hired as a meeting room.

The open camping field covers seven acres and is available to all scouting groups. It has toilets, showers and wash-places, with fresh-water taps on the field.

At the centre various courses for Leaders, Venture Scouts and Scouts are run throughout the year.

Details of the amenities and activities can be obtained from:

The County Secretary (Scouts),
47 North Bailey,
Durham, DH1 3ET.
Tel: 0191 386 4192

Moorhouse Woods

These woods are owned by the National Trust and are now a nature reserve, so you must take care when walking through them and obey the Country Code. By taking care you will be rewarded by the sighting of the variety of bird life that inhabits the woods, as well as rabbits and other wildlife.

The Railway Line

This divides Moorhouse camping site from Woodside Farm, and was part of the old East Coast Main Line from Newcastle, which joined the Pallion to Penshaw line after crossing the Victoria Viaduct near Cox Green (Ref. James Steel Park Walks).

Continuing South, on the East side of the River Wear, until just before reaching Carrville, a branch line swung off, to recross the river by the Belmont Viaduct (Ref. Kepier Walks North).

These lines and viaducts are no longer in use due to the re-routing of the North to South, East Coast Line, and because the A1M motorway bi-sected the Belmont section when it was built, leaving only parts of the embankment, which are now covered in grass and trees.

Public Houses

A number of public houses, including a motel, can be found within easy reach of the start of this walk, and all serve meals or bar snacks throughout the year.

Leaving the Rainton Lodge Motel, which stands on the left hand side of the road (A690), just up from the entrance to the scout camp at West Rainton, turn down to the left, taking the Finchale Priory signpost directions. You will find first the Masons Arms, which is just along the road which swings off to the right, while the Leamside is on the bend at the foot of the hill, on the road leading to Finchale Priory.

Should you have transport and wish to travel a couple of miles on, the Blacksmiths Arms in Low Pittington is the place to head for.

Opposite the Rainton Lodge, on the A690 Durham to Sunderland Road, look for the Pittington signpost. Follow this road and you will find the Blacksmiths at the bottom.

Re-furbished in 1995 to provide a comfortable bar where snacks are available, it also has a restaurant (with non-smokers area). Both have open fires to warm you on those cold days.

There is a Blackboard Special as well as the main wide-ranging menu, which includes fish, steaks, chicken, casseroles and vegetarian dishes.

The Blacksmiths Arms is open for food from 12 till 2.00 p.m. lunchtimes and from 6.30 p.m. every evening except Sundays, with a traditional Sunday lunch served, which at the time of our research cost £5.50 for the three courses.

Here you will be made most welcome by Audrey and Neville Rodgers, who run this lovely little village pub. Telephone number 0191 372 0287.

MOORHOUSE WALK

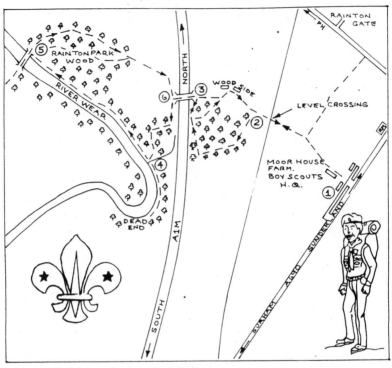

① LAYBY A690 GRID REF. 457316
② STRAIGHT OVER LEVEL CROSSING 200 METERS TURN LEFT.
③ TURN LEFT AND OVER BRIDGE.
④ AT BOTTOM OF STEEP STEPS TURN RIGHT.
⑤ TURN RIGHT AT FOOTBRIDGE AND UP STEEP CLIMB.
⑥ TURN LEFT OVER BRIDGE THEN RIGHT OVER FIRST STILE ON RIGHT HAND SIDE.

MOORHOUSE/RAINTON PARK WOODS

Distance: 5.22 km/3.25 miles

Walking Time: Two hours approx.

Conditions: Two steep, stepped inclines, some muddy paths
in wet   weather.

Pathfinder: 572

Grid Ref: 318 457

The long lay-by which lies alongside the A690 (Durham to
Sunderland) approximately three-quarters of a mile from the
Sunderland/Carrville A690 interchange on the A1M, is the starting-
point for this particular walk (1).

Double yellow lines prevent you from parking right up in the head
of the cul-de-sac, so you need to walk up past the Gardeners Cottage
on your left.   Then just beyond this lovely little cottage are the
gates leading into Durham County Scouts Moorhouse campsite.
Turn in through the white wrought-iron gates and follow the public
footpath signpost, which stands at the exit to the lay-by.

The path is wide and lined with trees, then a few yards to the left
lies the building belonging to the scouts.

Keep following the path down towards the railway crossing at the
bottom of the incline. However, before you reach the track, there
is a very faded notice up on the right stating "Footpath only, no
bicycles, horses or motor vehicles".

There is also a rather muddy section (after bad weather) which
needs to be negotiated. This can be done by walking carefully along
the grass verges. Not that you will damage the verge, more likely
you may find these water-logged as well.

Judging by the amount of rust, the railway line appears to be little
used, but as with all crossings of this type, be careful, look both
ways before crossing and keep looking as you cross.

Once safely over this, you will find the path drops slightly and you can see the huddle of buildings that make up Moorhouse Farm. You have no need to go through the farm itself as the path you follow goes off to the left about 100 yards from the railway crossing (2).

Once again this is a path which can be badly affected by wet weather, with this time the centre section being the drier.

This path takes you alongside a small wood which is owned by the National Trust and called Moorhouse Wood Nature Reserve. There is a notice to this effect on the fence around the wood, asking you to protect the wood and its inhabitants.

The path runs out into an open field, but just before this, another one goes off to the right and into the woods. Take this one.

This path is narrower and soft, but not muddy, as it winds its way through the trees.

Following the path to the right you come to a set of steps, then a slight incline, until you are above a small burn. Here you need to climb down to the bottom using the log steps set in the bank.

Crossing the burn should pose no problem as a wooden platform has been built on the far side, which you can step on to. Another set of steps goes up to the right, helping you to climb the short but steep incline. You may find that half way up there is a tree lying across the path, but it is easy to climb over.

The trunk has fallen across the path but not on it, which means you have to climb over what is a three-foot-high hurdle.

Once this obstacle has been negotiated, a continuation of the steps take you to the top of the bank.

Here at the top the path branches, and you need to follow the left-hand one, leading in the direction of the A1M motorway, which can be seen and heard through the trees.

Parts of the next section of the path can be muddy, probably only during wet or winter weather, and it is advisable to have a walking stick to give you extra support.

Following the path through the trees brings you to more wooden steps, where the path drops into and out of a hollow.

Then just before you reach the next branch in the path, you will see an old, fairly large tree at the side. See if you can identify it.

At the branch which is facing a fence, turn left towards the motorway, and here in the corner stands a stile. This leads into a grass field. Over the stile the going underfoot is soft but not too difficult to cross.

Straight in front of you there is a series of broad wooden steps leading up to the footbridge which spans the motorway at this point (3).

So it's up the steps, over the stile, turn left and across the bridge. Hang on to your hat as you do so, because even on the calmest of days, the up draft from the traffic flowing along underneath is enough to take it off your head and send it spinning down the motorway.

Once you have crossed over to the far side, you will find another stile to your left. Climb this, and drop down into the field, the site of the long disused Mallygill Quarry.

Skirting the field, keep the fence and motorway to your left, until you reach the point where the field and woods come together on the corner to your right.
Here you will find a path leading into the woods, with a sign at the entrance stating that you are now entering Moorhouse Woods.

This path follows the line of the fence around the field as you walk through the trees. Take care along this section of path, as the bank on your left drops steeply down to the small "Gill" which flows down in the River Wear.

Very shortly you reach the far end of the fence and corner of the field, after passing over a small wooden bridge along the way. Turn off to the left and continue along the path into the woods proper.

Those of you who have already done the Finchale Priory walk

(No. 8 in this book) will no doubt recognise the next section of this one, because just along from the corner of the field is what the authors found to be the ideal spot for a break. From here you can see through the trees, down to the floor of the valley and the River Wear as it rushes on its journey to the sea.

Passing on from here, you continue to follow the path as it descends to the river.

As the slope becomes steeper you will find that wooden steps have been built into the sides to assist, but do take care; even when climbing down you will still find them very steep, and there is a straight drop off to your left; and in winter time or after rain these steps can be very slippery.

Now, having climbed down to near the river's edge, take a look at the burn, and especially the floor and sides of it (4).

See how it has been inlaid with flat stones and a small wall built up at the sides, the purpose of this now long forgotten.

Now simply turn right and walk along the river path, keeping an eye out for the concrete block at the right-hand side of the path and the wooden posts sunk into the ground close to the river on the left-hand side. On the far bank you can see where the bank has been built up with stones.

As to whether these three points are connected, remnants of a bridge or quayside, the authors have been given various accounts, but unfortunately none have been substantiated. So they must, as far as this book goes, remain a mystery, as with the flat stone in the burn.

This section of the walk, which is also covered in Walk No. 8, is always very pleasant. The path is firm and level no matter what the weather.

Set in the river you will see a small island, a favourite resting place for the birds that inhabit the river, the mallard duck, waterhens and gulls. Then from here it is only a short distance to the footbridge that crosses the river at that point.

You do not cross the bridge, but turn up to the path on your right (5), leading up into what the National Trust have called Moorhouse

Woods, although the Ordnance Survey map shows it as Rainton Park woods.

The path climbs steeply out of the valley floor, with the help of steps cut into the bank side.

Once the path reaches the top, it runs alongside the fence of a field and is easily followed, till you reach the edge of the wood.

Looking over to your left you will see another National Trust sign for Moorhouse Woods, and a stile.

Over the stile, the path follows alongside a hedge. Keep this to your left and walk the length of the field, to bring you back on to the tarmac path and footbridge over the A1M motorway (6).

Once over this, it's over the stile on your right, down the steps, across the short stretch of grass and finally over the stile into the "Moorhouse Wood" Nature Reserve once again.

After climbing the stile, swing to the left and follow the path straight on, ignoring the right hand path, which you used on the way in.

The path you are following takes you deep into the woods but is easy to follow.

Coming up to the fence around the fields and yards which surround Moorhouse Farm, you will see the reason why the path shown on the Ordnance Survey map should be ignored.

At this point the path veers to the right. Watch out here for tree roots protruding through the path.

Down a small dip you go, up the steps and on to the path for a stretch before you emerge from the woods through an area of low shrubs and a small clearing. Around this point, see if you can spot the old tree with the hole in its trunk.

Leaving the path out of the shrubs, turn right, away from the farm and back to the railway crossing, remembering to watch both ways as you cross.

It is then just a matter of retracing your steps down the broad path, past the scout huts, up to the lay-by to finish off your walk.

POINTS OF INTEREST
KEPIER WOODS (NORTH)

Kepier Woods and Quarries

Kepier Woods stand on both banks of the river Wear to the north of Durham City. They are easily reached from the A1M motorway by way of the A690 Carrville link road into Durham, which runs alongside the woods for a short distance.

Site of the ancient quarries of Kepier, the woods hold a thousand or more years of Durham's history.

Stone hewed from the rock faces of the gorge that the river has carved for itself through this part of Durham was probably used not only on the Cathedral and Castle at Durham, but for many more grand buildings, churches and houses in the district.

While the woods, which are made up of various types of trees, including the English Oak, are a natural habitat for birds and squirrels, the river plays host to a variety of water-fowl and fish.

Walking through the woods today, it is hard to imagine the industrial activity that went on here until the 1930s, such as drift coal-mining and quarrying.

Evidence of this can still be found close to Michael's Crossing. When the water level is low, you can still see the concrete blocks which supported a rope bridge used by the miners to cross from Brasside into Kepier Woods, on their way to work in the drifts.

Coal from these drift mines, was most likely "tracked" up to the Grange Foundry and Ironworks, which stood close to what is now a municipal caravan site at Belmont, adjoining the A1M, and Maureen Terrace. Or could this have been Marine Terrace at one time (as suggested by W.M.C. Fawcett, in his Caldecotes Circular Walk leaflet), on account of the sea-going equipment produced by the foundry between 1867 and 1926?

Then in 1941 the Germans, who must have thought the site was still of some importance, dropped four bombs on it, although the area had been derelict for a good number of years by then.

Belmont Bridge

The viaduct which spans the river from Belmont to Brasside is another of those magnificent bridges that the Victorian engineers were so good at building.

Standing at 130 ft., it was the highest in England when it was opened in 1856.

Nine arches of 60 ft. span gave it a total length of 694 ft/230 metres.

It is of the same design as the North Road viaduct, which runs through Durham City.

The stone which went into the building of Belmont viaduct came from five separate quarries: Claxtons (Gateshead), Leam, Pensher (Penshaw), Benton (Newcastle) and the Roman Quarry at Rudchester, which is approximately two miles west of Heddon-on-the-Wall, on the B6318 Military Road out of Newcastle.

Not only stone went into the building of this viaduct but also:-

        250,000 cubic feet of ashlar
        119,000 cubic feet of rubble
        34,000 cubic feet of brickwork
        97,200 cubic feet of dry filling over the arches
        35,000 tons of lime.

The bricks were produced on site by steam-driven machinery, which leads us on to the mystery of the old brick buildings close to the viaduct and now in ruins.

Could these have been where the bricks were produced? There is what appear to be a boiler and kiln in one of the ruins. Or do the buildings have some connection with the drift mines?

The viaduct is now disused, after being in service for a good number of years, carrying the main East Line track, down from Newcastle into Durham and on to Bishop Auckland.

Known as the Belmont junction on the Bishop Auckland Branch line, this was dis-continued when a more direct link from Newcastle through the Team Valley (Gateshead) and Chester-le-Street, was brought into service.

When this happened, it was history repeating itself, as the Belmont line had replaced the old "Goods Line", which came down on the East side of the river, past what is now West Rainton, and terminating at Gilesgate Station.

The Durham goods line had only been open some 12 years when the new line over the Belmont viaduct opened. It had by coincidence been opened on the 18th June 1844, the 29th anniversary of the Battle of Waterloo.

Both lines were bisected by the building of the A1M motorway or at least the sites were. However, parts of the embankment of the Goods Line can still be seen as you leave the informal car-park and follow the path alongside the A690. This road follows the line of the old railway, which ended in the goods station at Gilesgate, now long gone into the pages of history.

Refreshments

Due to the location of this particular walk, lying between Rainton and Durham, the authors would suggest that you should, if you have transport, cross the A1M motorway, head for Rainton and try one of the three public houses listed in Walk No. 9 in this book.

Or head into Durham City, with its wider choice of places for refreshments, where we feel sure you will find somewhere to suit your own individual tastes.

KEPIER WOODS (NORTH)

Distance: 5.33 km/3.8 miles

Walking Time: 2 1/4 hours approx.

Conditions: Flat riverside and woodland paths; two steep inclines

Pathfinder: 572

Grid Ref: 292 439

Starting from a small car park at the north end of the Belmont road bridge (1), over the A690 (Carrville/Durham link road), this walk will be taking you down to the Northern end of Kepier Woods and back, passing through the sites of the ancient quarries of Kepier as you do so.

The pathway that you seek, to take you out of the car-park, lies to the road side, so turn your back to the woods and cross over to the left- hand corner.

Although narrow, the path is well defined and easy to follow as it runs parallel with the A690 road way.

It follows what was once the railway track and embankment of the old North Eastern Railway Co. line although apart from the steep slopes on either side, no other sign of that line remains.

Over to your left you are looking at the tops of old British oak trees growing in the woods along the river banks, while to your right are the newer North American red oaks, planted in the 1970's to shield the embankment from the road.

The road is a busy one, leading as it does to the A1M motorway and on to Sunderland, so that the traffic noise can be a little heavy at times.

The path does however draw away from the traffic as it goes down behind the embankment, which helps cushion the sound.

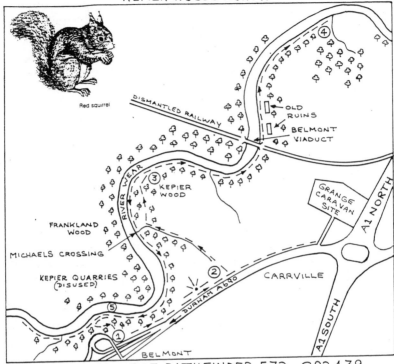

① CAR PARK GRID REF. PATHFINDER 572   292439.
② TURN
③ TURN RIGHT.
④ YOU COME TO THE END OF THE WOOD AND A STREAM
   TURN ROUND AND HEAD BACK FOLLOWING THE RIVER.
⑤ TURN LEFT AND FOLLOW PATH UP TO THE CAR PARK.

Kepier Hospital gatehouse

If you take this walk in early September, you will find the hedgerows laden with brambles ready for picking, but do allow yourself ample time if you should decide to go berry picking.

Follow the path with a fence and hedge to your left and the embankment to your right, until you reach a stile set into the fence (2).

At this point it is possible to see the large factories on the industrial estate across the A690.

Climb the stile, which did have a "Way" sign fastened to its posts at one time, and enter the field.

The path runs down the side of what begins as overgrown hedgerows and then develops into a burn, which runs through them.

This in turn becomes a "Gill" which plunges down the bank as it enters Kepier Woods, to pour into the River Wear on the valley floor, at Michael's Crossing.

Following this excellent all-weather path is easy. You can even use the line of iron 'man-holes' which run alongside it as a guide.

Just before you enter the woods, looking over to the left you can see how steep the Gill becomes. (The word Gill is taken from the Icelandic "gil", meaning a deep and narrow ravine, often wooded.)

You, however, continue to follow the path as it enters the woods, curving to the right and starting its own descent to the river below.

As you walk down you come to the first of five forks in the path.

At the first two of these, take the right-hand path; at the third, the wider left-hand one.

From here you can now see the river down at the base of the incline. Within 200 yards the fourth 'fork' appears; take the right-hand one again (the left drops down to the riverside path).

Passing a small tree on the corner, the path slopes slightly to the left for a short section, which demands extra care as you negotiate it, before reaching a wider part.

Then at last the fifth and final fork; this time take the left-hand trail.

This brings you out on to a broad, flat ledge, which has been carved out of the rock face that rises up to your right. Here a large tree, with its roots deeply embedded in the rock to support itself, has grown.

Just beyond this ledge you at last reach the path leading down. This has steps of a sort cut into it, but they are now beginning to erode.

So taking care, and this is where a walking stick comes in handy, you start your climb down.

Once at the bottom you will find the path almost disappears, as you turn to the right (3).

This is because the next part of the walk is over rocks and sand washed along by the river in times of flood water.

After only a short walk, the path becomes more visible as it rises a little above the flood water line, and apart from the tree roots which stick through the soil, the going becomes easier.

As you round the bend of the river, there, through the trees you can see the now, dis-used Belmont railway viaduct which carried the N.E.R.'s Bishop Auckland branch line.

Just before you reach the viaduct lie three large stones and a tree trunk across the path, but these can be passed with no problem, by climbing over them.

The path takes you through one of the arches of this, another monument to Victorian engineering.

Towering 400 metres/130 ft. above your head as you pass under it, you can only feel in awe of the men who built these structures.

Once through the viaduct you will find another three large stones obstructing the path, climbing over these even on a damp day, should be done with care.

There is also another fallen tree at this point, which needs to be either climbed over or under the choice is yours.

Then the last of the obstacles, is a really large tree, lying alongside the left hand side of the path, which in turn winds around the base of tree, that is, between the tree roots and the rock face.

Once around this you come to a cluster of ruined brick built constructions, one on the left of the path, the other two, on the right (see Local Interest Notes).

Within a few metres/yards, again on the right of the path you will see what appears to be a large sloping trough with brick walls.

The path at this point comes up to a stile, which you climb, taking you into open woodland, with a good level path to follow.

This area is covered in the summer months, with both the strongly scented "Himalayan Balsam" plant and one called with a variety of names e.g. "Lords and Ladies", "Cuckoo Pint" or "Jack in the Pulpit".

The latter plant can be see in late summer as a green stem containing red berries, beware the berries are poisonous.

Continuing along this path eventually brings you a fence running down the side of another "gill" running down into the river.

This fence is the limit of this walk, as beyond it, is private property (4).

So it is then only a matter of re-tracing your steps along the riverside path.

It is worth noting that from the start of the walk up to the turning point, will take just over an hour, without any long stops.

So bearing this in mind, leave yourself plenty of time for the return, part of which is along a different route.

Follow the path back to the point where you descended the hill to the river side (3).

This time don't go back up, but continue along the river side, until you reach the "gill" at Michael's Crossing.

It is here that you may be able to spot the old bridge supports in the river itself (concrete blocks).

This bridge was possibly the rope bridge that was used by the miners to cross from Brasside to Kepier Woods for work.

Once over the crossing the footpath improves rapidly and is very firm in all weathers.

All around you there is evidence of the quarrying that was carried out all those hundreds of years ago.

While remembering that stone from these quarries allowed the masons to carve and build the Cathedral and Castle in Durham, leaving their workmanship to be seen for all time, think about men who cut the rock with nothing but hand tools.

After a good walk along the river path, shaded by the trees, you reach a small bridge spanning a third and final "gill". This one has handrails on the river side (5).

Just beyond this particular landmark, you will find a tarmac path coming down the hill, on the left. This path will now take you back up the hill to the point at which you started this walk.

It is also the point at which you turn back on Walk No. 11.

Be prepared for a slow, steep climb, as the path curves its way up to the top, through the trees and then out into an open field in front of the car park.

We feel certain that you will agree with us that the climb is well worth the effort, after a peaceful walk through an area of woodland, which holds a thousand years of history.

Kepier Hospital as an inn

This was originally founded in 1112 A.D. by Bishop Flambard, on a site close to the church of St. Giles.

It can be assumed that it did not become known as Kepier until the hospital at St. Giles was burnt down and a new site was found near the river at what is now Kepier Farm.

The word Kepier is derived from two old English words meaning weir and fish trap ('Kepier Hospital' by Dorothy M. Meade).

Completed in 1180 A.D., the new hospital was at that time, the wealthiest in the country. It was run by some thirteen monks who performed practical tasks such as tanning, baking and milling as well as watching over fifteen old men, in what was not only a hospital but a church, dormitory hall and confessional court.

It is said to have been burnt down in 1306 by Scots raiders, but this is strongly disputed by Dorothy M. Meade, in her book 'Kepier Hospital' (see books for further reading).

Records show that there was no Scottish invasion in 1306, but in

1311 they constantly harried the North, until in 1312 Durham itself was attacked and set on fire, and in June 1315, goods belonging to the hospital were seized. This may have led, at a much later date, to people mistakenly attributing the fire also to the Scots.

Once more the hospital was rebuilt, only to be stricken by the "Black Death" in 1351, and then to be disbanded in 1545 as part of the Dissolution measures brought about by Henry VIII.

Built with what was probably local stone from the Kepier Quarries, as was Durham's Norman Cathedral, only the gate house of the hospital survives today.

In 1568, what was left of the hospital came into the hands of the Heath family, who constructed a mansion house on the site.

This eventually became an Inn for a long time during the early part of the 19th century. A photograph of this can be seen in a book called "Durham in Old Photographs".

Owned now by Mrs. Watson, the gate-house has been made habitable once more, with a new roof being fitted in 1995.

A walk through the arched doorway will take you through the rear of the building, and the farm house can be seen at the top of the rise.

Kepier Hospital gatehouse

Details of this are also covered in Dorothy M. Meade's excellent book, along with old photographs and sketches.

Brick and Tile Works

The arched, brick building, which stands to the right of the path leading away from the farm yard to the woods, is the only surviving remnant of a 19th- century brick and tile works which existed in the area. The 'kiln', for that was its original purpose, has had various functions in the years following the demise of the brickworks.

It is now surrounded by a number of odd electricity poles, which are part of the Northern Electricity Boards training ground. Had they been allowed, the Board intended, in 1944, to build a large power station, with 13 cooling towers on this very site.

So strong was the resistance, led by the Durham Preservation Society (founded 1942, now the City of Durham Trust), that the project was moved to Dunston-on-Tyne instead.

Quarries and Coal Mines

Throughout the woods ample evidence can be found of the quarrying that has been carried out there over the centuries, but very little if any can be found of the coal mining, which was being done up until the 1930s.

The best time to try to find any signs of these activities would of course be in the autumn or winter, when the leaves are off the trees and bushes and the vegetation is low.

Rifle Range

Along the edge of the river bank, at the bottom of the meadow, stand two, concrete walls. These are in fact the remains of what were once earth-covered rifle butts, which were part of the firing range that once occupied the site.

They first appeared on maps of 1896 and then again 1920, only to be omitted in 1939 (probably wartime restrictions).

It would appear that they were first used by the military during the Zulu and Boer wars in Africa, to train recruits, who would have been using Martine Henry rifles.

Evidence of this has been found around the site, in the shape of spent bullets of the type that this particular rifle used, standard issue for the British army at this period of its history.

It has been suggested that it is still possible to find these spent bullets around the site, even today.

The Mill

Kepier Mill, which was run from a watercourse or race, close to the gate-house (see map), stood until 1870 when it was destroyed by fire.

It took the borough firemen and fire engine some considerable time to reach the mill, and they were unable to save it.

The fire had been discovered at 2.45 pm on the 24th September and by 7.00 a.m. one of the walls finally collapsed, bringing an end to the fire.

It was never rebuilt, the ruins gradually disappearing until only an arch over the mill stream can be seen today, and then only when the vegetation is low.

Flora and Fauna

Parts of this walk cover over a thousand years of Durham's history, with seasonal changes for the nature lover, passing through wild meadow and woodland, along one of the most tranquil parts of the River Wear, where fish such as salmon, sea trout and chubb can be found, while the woods and hedgerows are the habitat of a variety of wild birds.

Who knows, you may even catch a glimpse of a squirrel among the leafy oaks in Kepier Woods.

Refreshments

With this walk starting close to the city itself we thought it better that readers made their own choice as to where they should seek refreshments, if they so wished, as a good number of various styles of tea shops, cafes or pubs can be found within the bounds of the city.

KEPIER WOODS (SOUTH)

Distance:	5.31 km/3.3 miles
Walking Time:	2 1/4 hours approx.
Conditions:	Flat and hilly woodland paths
Pathfinder:	572
Grid Ref:	274 429

Using the car park of the Durham Health and Activities Centre Skating Rink as a starting and finishing point of this Walk (1), you come out on to Freemans Place; turn left, away from the City and down to where the road comes to the junction with Providence Row.

Over to the left are the river and a strip of common land called the "Sands". Further down the road on the right-hand side stood Durham's Football Club. A new block of luxury flats and a cul-de-sac of new detached houses are now in its place.

Just beyond these the road becomes Orchard Road, which has a name plate at the head of it.

Running off to the left and close to the river there is a broad tarmac footpath.

Walk along this until you reach the old gate house of Kepier Hospital.

A plaque set up in the wall gives you a potted history of the building (for a more detailed history see the list of recommended books at the back of this one).

Just past the gate-house there is a tubular barred gate with barbed wire around the top, so make sure you use the stile at the left hand side.

Follow the narrow tarmac path across to the other gate which has its stile at the right hand side this time.

KEPIER WOODS SOUTH

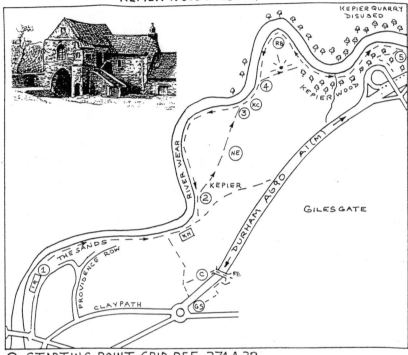

① STARTING POINT GRID REF 274429
② TURN RIGHT.
③ TURN RIGHT ONCE OVER THE STILE.
④ TURN RIGHT.
⑤ STOP AND TURN ROUND AT FOOT OF STEEP INCLINE AND
 FOLLOW RIVER PATH BACK TO THE START.
N.E NORTH EASTERN ELECTRICITY BOARD TRAINING CENTRE
RB RIFLE BUTTS.
KH KEPIER HOSPITAL.
KC KEPIER COLLIERY.
GS GILSGATE STATION NOW ARCHIBALDS.
C OLD CHAPEL OF THE HOSPITAL OF ST MARY
 MAGDALENE 1457.

This puts you on to a path which runs past the farm yard and then out on to a concrete roadway (2).

Keeping the field to your left and the cluster of electricity poles to your right, continue straight down this roadway until you reach the far end (3). Here you will find two stiles next to each other, at the left-hand side. You take the one which goes straight into the field in front of you, not the one that goes off to the left.

The track here can be very muddy in wet weather, even though some attempt has been made to strengthen it with large rocks.

It dips down gently before coming out on to an open area, and rising again. Climb up the far side through the space between the bushes towards a steel barred gate (4).

Once at the top walk straight into the grassy field, keeping the fence and hedge to your right hand.

Before you proceed too far along this section, look back if it is a fine, clear day. Here you will get a different view of Durham Cathedral and Castle from the normal picture postcard ones, while down at the bottom meadow the River Wear twists its way through the landscape on its voyage to the sea.

In one corner of the field, close to the river, stand two concrete walls, all that is left of what were target "butts" of a long disused rifle range (R.B.), while over the fence behind you, as you look towards the river, lies the site of what was Kepier Colliery (K.C.), now long gone, as are the rest of the coal mines and quarries that dotted the area in the 18th and 19th centuries.

As you follow the hedge and fence, bringing you close to the river, you reach the far end of the field, where you will find another stile with two heavy upright, wooden posts.

Once over this stile you are in "Kepier Woods", and here the firm all-weather path closely follows the banks of the river.

The woods, especially in spring and summer, are carpeted with wild flowers such as white wood anemones, yellow lesser celandine, bluebells and daffodils, while the river is home to a variety of waterfowl, mallard ducks, coots and water hens, as well as gulls. The trees are home to the crows, tits and other woodland birds.

A little way into the woods a culvert or "gill" comes down from the hillside on your right, cutting across the path, but it is easily crossed, as large rocks have been set in to form steps down and across. The trees provide welcome shade from the sun on a warm summer's day.

Continue along the path until you reach a point where a tarmac path joins it from the right (5). This path comes down from the car park situated just off the slip road to Carrville on the A690 (Carrville Link Road) after you leave the A1M motorway.

It is in fact the starting-point of another of the walks (Kepier Woods North) featured in this book, and can be an extension of this walk, for those who have the time.

However, as we have tried to limit the walks to no more than 2-2 1/2 hours duration, we have split this particular section, giving two separate walks.

And so, for the purposes of this particular walk, you now have to turn about and re-trace your steps, but only as far as the entrance to the woods. Here, when you have climbed the stile back into the meadow, swing sharp right and follow the path along the banks of the river. This takes you around behind the old rifle butts at the bottom of the field.

At the end of this section you find yourself back on familiar ground, the bushy area in the depression. Here, at the far side, you come up to the double stile you saw on the way in. Climb the first, and this time step on to and over the one off to your right (3).

The path here is not very wide, but it is easy to follow, with a chain link fence and concrete posts on your left and the river over to the right beyond the vegetation.

Over the fence lies a field with football and rugby pitches.

See if you can spot the little fishing platform on the far side of the river.

At about the half-way stage of this stretch of path, you reach what was once a "kissing gate", and the start of a rough pasture field with wire strand fencing. It is in this field that you can watch the house martens darting and swooping, as they feed off the flying insects, in the spring-time.

From the gate round to the barred gate and stile in front of Kepier Hospital is approximately 400 metres, which allows you an unrestricted view of the river.

Then simply by following the tarmac path, you are on your way back to the "Rink".

A short diversion over the "Sands" will allow you to walk alongside the river, till you reach the end of what we hope you have found to be a peaceful and interesting walk.

POINTS OF INTEREST
MOUNT JOY/DURHAM CITY

Baths Bridge and Swimming Baths

The bridge which takes you across the River Wear, at the foot of Pelaw Leazes, to the swimming baths on the far side, is in fact the third to stand on this site.

An arched, wooden structure was the first, built in the middle part of the nineteenth century. It linked for the first time the two most historic parts of the city, Gilesgate and Elverts.

This stretch of the river, with its tree-lined banks, was always a popular point for the oldest regatta in the country.

Giving access to the swimming baths on the Elvert side of the river, this first bridge was replaced in 1894 by a wrought iron, latticed profile structure, at a cost of £700. This latticed profile was a familiar Durham landmark to visitors seeking the pleasant picnic sites along the river banks.

It became known as the "Baths Bridge", as against "Pelaw Leazes Bridge", the name by which its predecessor had been known. Then, by the time it too needed to be replaced, it was "Old Baths Bridge". The present arched, concrete bridge, built nearer the shape of the original, was opened in June 1962.

When the public 'Baths' were opened by Lord Barrett, in 1855, they comprised public wash-houses and two ponds 49 feet 6 inches long by 19 feet 6 inches wide, with a maximum depth of 4 feet 6 inches.

Now whether these "ponds" were for swimming or for washing clothes is in dispute. As one source of information points out, there was no swimming pool as such on the site at that time, while a public notice announcing the opening of the Baths gives the details of the "ponds".

What is certain is that in 1932 on the 28th September the present building was opened as a swimming pool.

Ancient Fort

The hill known as Maiden Castle was the focus of an archaeological dig in 1956, as it is believed to have prehistoric origins, possibly Bronze or Iron Age.

Agricultural College

In 1921 the County Council of Durham realised the need for a farming centre, and so bought the Houghall Estate from Durham University. A total of 476 acres was acquired, of which 380 acres became farm, the rest being used for other purposes.

The School of Agriculture was finally established in 1938, comprising four sections: Farm, Dairy, Horticulture and Poultry units, with residence for 72 students.

Since then it has gone from strength to strength and is now world-famous.

Botanic Gardens

While the University of Durham's Botanic Gardens are not on the path of this walk, they are only a minute's diversion away, at the top of a very steep climb and, if you are a keen gardener, they are well worth taking a look at.

On the premises, you will find a tea room which serves hot and cold drinks as well as light snacks, and for those with their own food, if it's a fine day, there is a picnic area. Toilet facilities cater for the disabled and able-bodied.

The Botanic Gardens moved to this eight-hectare site from Stockton Road, Durham, in 1970, under the guidance of Professor Donald Boulter.

This was the first garden in the country to reflect the environmental concerns of the later twentieth century. Trees and plants grow together as they would be found in the wild. Conservation is the main theme in the management at the garden, which provides for educational and research projects.

To find out in more detail about the Botanic Gardens you can purchase a detailed leaflet at the reception desk, or ring/write to

Jo Cobb,
Horticultural Officer,
The Durham Botanic Officer,
University of Durham,
Hollingside Lane, South Road,
Durham DH1 3TN.
Tel: 0191 374 2671

Opening times:

The Garden Glasshouses: daily 9.00am till 4.00pm

The Visitors centre: 10.00am - 5.00pm every day April to October

1.00 pm - 3.30 pm every day November to March (weather permitting)

No dogs except guide dogs are admitted to these gardens.

Saint Oswald's Church

Standing in Church Street, St. Oswald's is the oldest and grandest of all the city's churches.

It was probably founded in 1150 A.D., with the North aisle of Saint Margaret being added in 1195 A.D.

An Anglo-Saxon cross shaft and finial of late 10th or early 11th century, were found and re-used in the church walls.

St. Oswald's was preceded by the Cathedral by only 17 short years, which gives a good indication as to the dominance of the church over the people's lives at that time.

Kingsgate Bridge

The bridge was completed in 1963 to link University buildings.

The innovative design by Ove Arup and Partners involved the bridge being built in two halves parallel to the river banks which were then turned to be locked into position over the river.

Kingsgate is the old name of Bow Lane, which runs down beside St. Martin-the-Bow church.

Boat House

Brown's boat house stands right on the banks of the river close to Elvert Bridge, on what is Feardon Walk.

From here you can hire rowing boats for river outings, or book a trip on the "Prince Bishop", a pleasure boat which plies the river.

Refreshments

Once again, as in the two previous walks (10 and 11) the authors are reluctant to name any particular cafes, public houses or restaurants, because of the number that exist in and around Durham City.

We feel it would be unfair to give our choice, when it is not possible for us to have tried each and every one.

So we leave it up to the reader, and we are sure that somewhere you will be able to find a place that pleases.

The Houghall Stiles, looking into the woods

MOUNT JOY DURHAM CITY

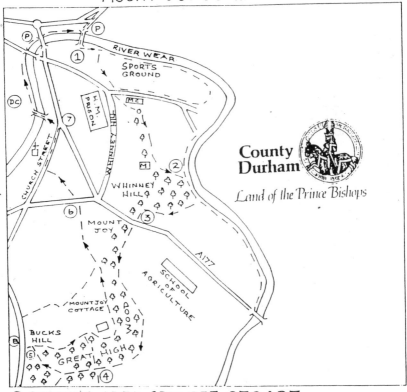

Ⓟ PARKING AREA GRID REF 279427.
① OVER FOOT BRIDGE TURN LEFT.
② TURN RIGHT.
③ CROSS OVER BUSY ROAD BE CAREFUL
④ STRAIGHT ON.
⑤ TURN RIGHT AT TOP OF HILL.
⑥ STRAIGHT OVER ROAD AND DOWN NARROW LANE.
⑦ TURN LEFT OVER THE BRIDGE AND DOWN THE
　　STEPS ON LEFT HAND SIDE.
DC DURHAM CATHEDRAL
NCP MUNICIPAL CAR PARK.
MC MAGISTRATE COURTS.
M SITE OF MAIDEN CASTLE.

MOUNT JOY / DURHAM CITY

Distance:	6.4 km/4 miles
Walking Time:	Two hours approx.
Conditions:	Flat and hilly paths, pavements.
Pathfinder:	572
Grid Ref:	278 427

Where to say a particular walk will start is usually determined by the type of transport that is used, and in most cases these days it is the motor-car.

So in choosing the starting-point for this walk around the outskirts of Durham City, we decided that as good a spot as any was the footbridge across the river leading to the old swimming baths in Elvert (1).

This bridge is at the foot of Pelaw Leazes, which is a short road going off to the left just past the roundabout on the A690 (Carrville Link Road) leading into Durham City, the Carrville Link Road being the dual carriageway from Sunderland across the A1M motorway.

It is possible sometimes to find room to park on Pelaw Leazes. However, if not it means going down into the N.C.P. multi-storey car park, which is situated further down the hill. This would then entail a short walk along the river bank to the bridge.

So, once at the bridge, you proceed to cross the river to the far side (1), where you turn left along the river footpath, passing the swimming baths and then the toilets on your right.

The toilets are open all year round and have disabled facilities.

Pass the privet hedge that surrounds the small bowling green, turning right at the corner, with the children's play area over to the left.

Follow the path, which is very firm and good for walking on, then veer up the slight incline until you almost reach the tubular barrier, swinging sharp right and up the steps in front of you.

Once up these, you are now at the foot of Whinney Hill, with its junction with Green Lane. The entrance to Durham Prison is just up the hill to the right. At this point you need to cross the road towards the Magistrates' Courts. Walk through the iron gates; this is a right of way, even through it passes through court grounds.

You eventually reach a large circular car park set in front of University student accommodation.

Here at the right hand side of the car park you find a path of tarmac, skirting the rear of the flats.

This tarmac path quickly turns into a hard soil one, just before you reach a 'Y' junction, at which one road leads off on to playing fields. Take the right-hand one leading towards a wooden barred gate and stile.

Ignore the stile and just follow the path through Maiden Castle Wood. Easy to follow, the path has steep wooded sides on the right and a fence to the left.

As you round the end of the woods, with the path now close to the river, the hillside above you is known as Maiden Castle, the site of a promontory (headland) fort (2).

Once around this hill side you reach another junction in the path, one route taking you along the river bank to a small cantilever footbridge.

The other - the one you need to follow - veers off to the right and past a kissing gate on the left. This path meanders through a tree lined avenue, with woods on the right and a cricket ground over the fence to the left for the next quarter of a mile or so, before you eventually come to the A177 roadway (3).

This has to be crossed with care, as up to the right there is a sharp bend and the traffic is inclined to be fast.

Directly over the road, the path continues, passing along the base of Mount Joy on the right and the School of Agriculture over the fence to the left.

The path is marked in places by horse and cycle tracks, so do be wary and keep a sharp look out for both.

Another thing to watch out for, at weekends, is the hordes of Saxons and Danes marauding through the woods, these being some of the re-enactment societies, who use the woods for their battles.

About 400 yards or so into this section from the road, the path starts to climb, and underfoot it becomes softer, which could present problems after wet weather.

The woods remain on your right, with the School of Agriculture's storage yard down to the left, until you reach the bend as the path curves around the hillside.

Here you will spot, on the left, a stile and then a field with railings round it. Painted on the railings there is a large red and white arrow.

The field belongs to Houghall Farm, and once you reach this point a small culvert cuts across the path. You will see on the left steps leading down to the stile.

A Way sign is attached to the fence, and an information board in the field tells you the background to what is known as the Houghall Discovery trail (4).

Just beyond the culvert, up on the path, there is a wooden seat, which makes a good place to take a half-way break, unless you want to carry on for a little longer and take your break in the Botanic Gardens.

Leaving the seat, follow the path once again, until you reach a fork. Here, at the top of a slight incline, you will find a signpost. While the one pointing to the right is showing you the direction to the Botanic Gardens, the other arm is unmarked. It does in fact take you to Pinnock Hill.

You are following the one to the right, so prepare yourself for a steep climb, as this incline must be rated as at least a one in six gradient. It is not for the faint-hearted, but it can be done in stages, and here is where a stick comes into its own.

At the top, your route takes you to the right, unless you wish to walk over to the left, on to and across Hollingside Lane to visit the Botanic Gardens (5) (see Points of Interest). Following the path to the right takes you along the top of Great High Woods.

It is now a simple matter of following the broad path as it skirts along the tree-line of the woods. It does narrow down at one point, just before it passes under an archway of holly bushes, and care should be taken for the steep slope off to the right.

Soon you reach what is the rear of Mount Joy Cottage, and here you turn sharp left.

It is worth noting the trees in this small area seem to be covered in ivy, and it is not unusual to see one or two with it wrapped around their trunks. All of them are well covered.

The path emerges from the woods in front of the gate to the cottage, and here you must turn right and down the "dolomite" path as it descends to Durham City.

Over to your left are the Science Laboratories of Durham University, and to your right, the woods.

Down towards the bottom of the incline stands Mount Joy House, just off to the right.

From here you have a magnificent view across the Parish of St. Oswald's to the Cathedral, one slightly different from the usual picture postcard. Instead of the front you can see the rear or far side (6).

By now you are walking on a broader, concrete path, which will bring you down on to the A1051 (Stockton Road).

Once again you will need to cross what is a very busy road, so do so with care.

Over on the far side, there is a narrow lane (School Lane) which runs down between the old cemetery wall on the left and the backs of houses on the right, emerging on to the A1050 (Church Street), between a children's play area and Saint Oswald's Infants' School.

Here once again you need to exercise caution as you cross to the footpath at the far side.

Turn right and walk past Saint Oswald's Church, continuing until you reach Dunhelm House, which is the newer concrete building on the left.

You need to turn left from Church Street, on to the forecourt of Dunhelm House, and over to Knightsgate Bridge, following the sign for "Cathedral and Heritage Centre" (7).

As you cross the bridge, look for the brass expansion joints, which allow the concrete to move in different temperatures. See how they are marked off, allowing the engineers to record the degree of movement.

At the far side of the bridge, steps head up to Bow Lane, this leading on into North Bailey, which runs below the Cathedral.

You go up the steps, but turn left at the top and descend, via another set of rather old steep stairs, to the riverside path.

Turn left and under the bridge along the footpath as it follows the river.

You pass the old boat house, with its roof level with the path, and after a short walk, go under Elvert Bridge.

Tucked into the corner of the bridge there is a set of stone steps which will take you up into the City Centre.

If however you are to finish your walk from where you set out, pass Brown's Boat House and stroll along till you pass under the A177 concrete bridge and up to the Baths Bridge.

Of course, if you parked in the N.P.C. car park, all you need to do is cross over the coach park beside Browns Boat House and into the car park.

So, at the end of this walk we hope you may have seen a little piece of Durham City that you may not have enjoyed before and also some of the lovely countryside that surrounds it.

Recommended Reading

Walk No.	Title	Author	ISBN	Date
1,2&3	Sunderland (River & Town) (A History from 1780s to Present)	A. C. Newton	1873138032	1993
1,2,3, 4 & 5	A message from Sunderland (A Portrait in old postcards)	Vincent Gordon	187078911	
1,2,3, 4 & 5	The River Wear (Photographs)	Tyne & Wear County Council Museums	0905974166	1984
4	The story of the Lambton Worm	Albert Hind		1978
6 & 7	Picture postcards of Chester-Le-Street	J.B. Stockoe & D.A. Hall	9028845038/CP	1988
7	More Crimes of Yester Year			
8	Animal Myths of Durham	A.C. Newton	1873138032	1993
8	The Tragedy of Finchale Priory (obtainable from the Priory)	J.F. Smith		
10	Durham Book of Antiquity (Vol 1 & 10)	Durham Reference Library		
10	Kepier Hospital	Dorothy Meade	0946105103	1995
10, 11 & 12	Durham as it Was	Ian Nelson A.L.A.		1974
10. 11 & 12	Durham County and City (with Teesside)	John C. Dewdney		
10, 11, & 12	Durham, the People and the Places (1914/1939)	Michael F. Richardson	1870268199	1994
12	Durham in old Photographs	June Crosby	0862996171	1990
12	Durham, Historic and University City	Margot Johnson MA & ELA		
	The Concise British Flora in Colour	W. Keble Martin	07181 14175	
	The Birds of Britain and Europe	Hermann Heinzel, Richard Fitter & John Parslow	**Paperback** 0-00219210-1 **Hardback** 0-00219234-9	
	Pathfinder Maps 550, 562 & 572.			